SO YOU WANT TO BE A LEADER?

Advice and Counsel to Young Leaders

2nd Edition

Dr. James H. Benson, Sr.
Colonel, USMC (Ret)

Order this book online at www.trafford.com
or email orders@trafford.com

Most Trafford titles are also available at major online book retailers.

Printed in the United States of America.

ISBN: 978-1-4251-4736-5 (hc)
ISBN: 978-1-4251-1628-6 (sc)
ISBN: 978-1-4251-6141-5 (e)

Trafford rev. 12/19/2012

 www.trafford.com

North America & international
toll-free: 1 888 232 4444 (USA & Canada)
phone: 250 383 6864 ♦ fax: 812 355 4082

SO YOU WANT TO BE A LEADER?

Advice and Counsel to Young Leaders

2nd Edition

Dr. James H. Benson, Sr.
Colonel, USMC (Ret)

DEDICATED

*Dedicated to the cadets and alumni of
Marion Military Institute who have
chosen a rigorous and noble path
knowing that it may lead
them into harm's way
And
to the Marines of Company "I",
3rd Battalion, 1st Marines whom
I served with in the Republic
of Viet Nam in 1969–70.
We fought together, suffered together,
grieved together,
and defeated a determined enemy
day after day.*

ACKNOWLEDGEMENTS

So You Want to be a Leader IS A BOOK CREATED OVER YEARS OF OBSERVATION OF THE HUMAN CHALLENGE, PERSONAL ERROR, AND THE COLLECTION OF DATA THAT I THOUGHT COULD HELP YOUNG LEADERS AS THEY ATTEMPTED TO HELP OTHERS ACHIEVE SUCCESS. There are those along the way who have made it possible for me to complete this task among the many distractions.

I must acknowledge my wife, Mary, whose grace, loyalty, and support were instrumental. Likewise, I must acknowledge my children, Catherine and Jim, who fortunately possess more of their mother's traits than mine. Both possess a spirit that I admire and treasure.

There were many in the United States Marine Corps who were models of competence and integrity and who taught me much about how to lead. Some include General Carl Mundy, General Butch Neal, Lieutenant General Paul Van Riper, and Lieutenant General Hank Stackpole. However, two of the finest officers and the ones I credit most were Colonel John Keith, Jr., former Commanding Officer of Marine Barracks, Subic Bay, Republic of the Philippines, and Colonel Gordon Batcheller, former Commanding Officer, 2nd Battallion, 7th Marine Regiment.

Dr. Phillip C. Stone, President of Bridgewater College, Bridgewater, Virginia is a leader that I admire and whose friendship I value. He offered me a job as his Executive Assistant that led to nine special years at Bridgewater College and the presidency that I now enjoy.

Coach Ray Bussard, the "Lone Eagle," great coach and friend, who remains an inspiration to me and hundreds of his high school and University of Tennessee athletes.

The Marion Military Institute Board of Trustees who gave me the opportunity to be the president of this great old school.

A special thanks to Elaine Dellinger, Tamara Brewer, Shawna Turner, and Merrrily Thompson whose ideas, edits, patience, and administrative support made this book possible.

My high school and college coaches who saw more potential in me than most of my teachers.

My grandmother, Hazel A. Hewitt, who gave me my core values.

To these, I am truly grateful.

"We should remember that one man
is much the same as another,
and that he is best
who is trained
in the severest school."
THUCYDIDES

SO YOU WANT TO BE A LEADER

Book Reviews

So You Want to be a Leader: Advice and Counsel to Young Leaders
Col. James H. Benson, Sr. USMC (Ret.)
Trafford, 147 pages, (paperback) $18.95, 978-142511628-0
(Reviewed: July, 2012)

What does it take to be a leader? Why do some people succeed, while others, despite intellect, credentials or experience, do not? Are leaders born or made?

These and many more questions are raised-and answered—by Col. James H. Benson's compendium of advice, comprised of quotes and stories from sources that include the classics, history, philosophy, literature, and, appropriately enough, the words of successful business leaders. All this is enlivened and exemplified by his experience as a highly decorated Marine officer, Viet Nam combat veteran, and president of a venerable Alabama military academy.

The Colonel takes his mission of making leaders seriously, noting that "leadership is not an end state but a process," that can be embraced and developed. The book's 46 accessibly-written entries, ranging in length from a single paragraph to four pages, address the issues, skills, challenges, strategies, wisdom and beliefs necessary for understanding the sources and practices of leadership basics, including: courage, integrity, power vs. authority, attitude, self-esteem, vision, values, acceptable failure, drive, tenacity, delegating, picking one's battles, commitment to learning, efficiency, public speaking, being a winner, et al.

Along with inspiring citations from Thucydides to Dale Carnegie, and Lincoln to Tom Peters, there is so much thoughtful, illuminating and original Benson material here, e.g.: "Good leaders are intense: real good leaders are passionate; but great leaders are predators when it comes to winning on the battlefield, the gridiron, or in the workplace."

Coaches, teachers, administrators, employers, pastors, and youth activities directors will find this useful and encouraging volume neither pedantic nor preachy, but a real resource.

Amazon.com Reviews

Very inspirational. Easy to read with lots of memorable quotes cited to correspond with chapters. Short chapters so you can read under any schedule. Would make an excellent reference book for any leader's library. Col Benson has a strong grasp of what it takes to be the most effective leader possible and does a good job of translating his experience into guidance for both novice and seasoned leaders. Makes reference to many of the techniques and strategies from a number of America's premier experts on leadership so this one book gives a glimpse into a diversity of writings. Written from a military (U.S. Marine Corps) point of view so the advice stresses ethics, honor, discipline, and getting the maximum results with the simplest efforts. Col Benson is now a college president and also has some interesting observations on academia. We passed this book through our family and every one of us found it to be a rewarding read. CS

_____

While this is truly a book for young leaders, there is much in it for even the most seasoned warrior. Colonel Benson does a masterful job helping the reader understand the challenges and opportunities a leader faces and how to best cope with them. While the book is a great vehicle for learning about the "principles of leadership," it also is very instructive about the two other aspects of team building—followership and membership. I like the way the author integrates quotes, short vignettes, and personal experiences and relates them to key attributes of successful leadership in this very readable book. If you are training or mentoring young leaders you should encourage them to read this book as part of their professional development. It will be a great investment in their future. RHE

This is a great book to read for anyone striving to become a leader. It teaches us a lot more than just being a military leader, but a successful leader in everything we do. Great book! KRB

I've been in the military for over 10 years and, of course, I tend to fall into the trap of thinking leadership "yeah, I got it" all the time. I still learn daily from the challenges of being a military commander, and I will never fall into the trap of thinking there is not something new to learn. This book helped reinforce the hard lessons I have learned and taught me to always look forward to seek self improvement.

I was very impressed with Col Benson's ability to bring together so much quality information and references to put together an outstanding guide to leadership. From his experience as a young platoon commander in Vietnam, his professional challenges throughout his distinguished military career, and his experience in the professional world, he has brought not only credibility but hard fought experience to bear on a very challenging subject.

I highly recommend this book to all leaders. It's now required reading for my subordinate commanders. AD

A must read.

I write this as the holiday season approaches. This book would be a wonderful gift to yourself or a loved one. It is a relatively quick read and is organized into 47 short chapters. Each chapter is well named to enhance a quick reference of a precise leadership skill. Col Benson has spent 40+ years in a leadership role: teacher, coach, military officer, and college administrator.

He is now the President of Marion Military Institute in Marion, Alabama. Colonel Benson alludes to the leadership mistakes he observed and made along the way. We all can learn from the mistakes of others and not repeat them.

I especially enjoyed the quotes at the beginning of each chapter, e.g., "Good leaders are intense; real good leaders are passionate; but great leaders are predators when it comes to winning on the battlefield, the gridiron, or in the workplace."

Thanks for the wisdom shared from a career Marine who "has been there and done that." EYM

---

5 Stars. Easy to read and great insight into what it takes to be successful. Focuses on leadership style, decision making process and importance of well defined core values. The author is right on target! A must read for all aspiring leaders at all levels. ELK

Col Benson has done an outstanding job in sharing his experience as a combat Marine, regimental commander, vice president of Bridgewater College and president of Marion Military Institute and the relationships these positions had in developing leadership qualities. Col Benson uses a common sense approach that "deals with personal experience and observations as an officer in the USMC" this quote taken from his introduction is why one would buy the book. Col Benson IS A LEADER, not only that but a man that leads by example and above all holds himself accountable for developing leaders under his charge. I highly recommend this book to military personnel, school teachers, coaches and anyone else wanting information on what it takes to be a leader in today's world!!! MB

This book was very insightful; I would recommend it to anyone who would like to try for the distinctive title of military leader. GBG

Barnes and Noble Reviews

I would rate "So You Want to Be a Leader?" up there with "The Art of War" and "The Book of Five Rings." Colonel Benson speaks from first hand experience. This book should be on the required reading list for leaders of all levels, civilian and military. Anonymous

James Benson's "So You Want to Be a Leader" is a relevant, thought-provoking guide that each parent should read and discuss with their children. The book is easy to read, chock full of useful, well-chosen quotations, and is a useful tool for any young person who wants to succeed in our fast-changing world. Benson applies the no-nonsense values and ethics of a combat Marine officer, coupled with the commonsense, compassion and mentoring spirit of a teacher and coach, to deliver a splendid guide for surviving and leading in a demanding society. From the battlefield, to the athletic field, to the college president's office, the advice and counsel that Benson offers to readers of all ages transcends all boundaries. I gave copies of this great book to my sons (26 and 24), and we continue to underline and discuss lessons each time we meet. I strongly recommend this composition to anyone who aspires to maximize their effectiveness at any important undertaking. Anonymous

Letters/Other Reviews

Well Pilgrim, you are bright, driven, moral, and watch the skyline at all times for possible trouble. You are a very rare bird. Your point about not just solving problems, but heading them off is worth the price of your book. Superb work Marine. JH

Thank you for giving me a copy of your book. I read it cover to cover and intend to read it again and keep it near as a handy reference. I think the book not only applies to "young leaders" but leaders at all levels. KPA

Thanks for the fabulous book. Of course, I recognize all you mention in there, especially my good friends Generals Krulak and Draude. Well done – a great book and Christmas present. SC

WOW! Love the template – in and out of many chapters that are short and sweet. Feel like I am reading your life's experiences in lessons learned. Hal Moore and I will love talking this through. Jim, the photo of you on page 75 – love it. Looks like Hal from 1965. Please do not under value this work. It works for all of us still open to learning. May we both serve another on another day! TMHM

Anyone who reads your great book would be sure to thank you right away. Therefore, you know that I have just started reading it. What a wonderful work! BG

Just got finished reading "So You Want to be a Leader" by retired Col Jim Benson. I read a lot of books each year and this was one of the few that was straight to the point and packed from cover to cover with useful information. RE

Personal letters/reviews

While most of my reading these days is in the spiritual area, I cannot tell you how much I benefitted and thoroughly enjoyed your book . . . You will find enclosed copies of 4 pages with my red underlining items that are of extra value and interest to me. As you can see, there was indeed a lot of red ink as well as red stars. JRW

Exceptional! Insightful! Interesting! So many leadership books are written as "academic exercises" and don't really offer much for serious practitioners. Your book is different, as it is written by a leader for people who lead. Very helpful! HMH

Your book is splendid. I have been there. IDM

"So You Want to Be a Leader" is an outstanding primer on leadership and I am having my two sons read it this summer. There are so many insights and just good common sense approaches to leadership . . . . Your book would serve as a base textbook for a course on leadership. SM

I am reading "So You Want to Be a Leader," and I think it is well-written . . . , contains some great insights for the leader. I also want my son to read it as he is at a place in his career where these issues come up daily, and he would benefit greatly from your thoughts and insights. RC

I am currently reading Colonel Benson's book, "So You Want to Be a Leader," and am thoroughly enjoying it. I recommend it for both pleasure reading and self-improvement. It is a very easy read and filled with wisdom we can use in practical very day life. Anonymous

---

"So You Want to Be a Leader" is an outstanding book on leadership. It is superbly done and reflects a lifetime study of the subject. JCB

I read your book this morning. I also have learned many of the same things that you have through trial and error in my own career. The book is a great read and contains very sound thinking. It should be a required read for anyone going into the coaching field. I wish I had read it 40 years ago; it certainly would have made me a better coach. It will be a proud and permanent fixture in my library. WFD

I just finished reading "So You Want to Be a Leader." It is a wonderful book. I sent it to my oldest son to read also. He graduates this year from Columbia University and hopefully, it will give him some direction for the future. RL

I just finished reading your book on the plane. What a great gift to young people! I made numerous notations while reading it, shared some of the most notable with my sons. Your thoughts directly support many of the value-based discussions that I have had with my boys. What you write about is exactly what our youth need to hear. Your work is certainly not to be restricted to young people seeking careers in the military, but should be read and discussed by parents and their children, regardless of goals and aspirations. I'll go back to it again and again to emphasize what leadership is all about. EB

"So You Want to Be a Leader" is superb. I finished reading it last night and will use the Chamberlain quote in my remarks at my 80th birthday party. WHT

"So You Want to Be a Leader" was great reading and my wife Debbie, is now reading it. She is a manager and says it is wonderful and will apply the lessons to her position. EK

"So You Want to Be a Leader" is an outstanding treatise on leadership. Future leaders will find this book a wonderful resource. I found therein many gems of wisdom. EAF

"So You Want to Be a Leader" is a great book! I wish it had been available in 1950 when I went to Korea as a brand new second lieutenant – straight out of West Point – without even a battery officer's guide. And, this book is full of what every cocksure West Point/Air Force/Navy graduate should know. Each chapter is a gem! MH

"So You Want to Be a Leader" should be required reading for young officers in the combat arms. The author has done a masterful job integrating "real world" examples and meaningful quotes into a very readable text. Well done! RE

WOW! Outstanding book on leadership. I have recommended it to the United States Weight-lifting Association and body. It is out there for others to read and refer to. MB

I am a big believer in self-improvement. Although I have mastered the computer in pretty much every way . . . my people skills have been lacking. Because of this, I have been reading many of the self-improvement books on the market. This book contains some of the best ideas I have read. I wish I would have read it a long time ago. WR

Anyone who reads your great book will be sure to thank you right away. What a wonderful work! BG

Your book is inspirational and your counsel invaluable. My wife and I had a project of reading it out loud. MHD, Jr.

After reviewing your website, I found your book, and I am happy to say I invested the time to read it. As a business manager and parent of a son who plans on entering the service as an officer your book really hits home for me. I am so glad I got it. RF

Jim, I finished your book in the flight back to the Naval Academy. Great read with many good points. I am always learning. EW

"So You Want to Be a Leader" contains great counsel to aspiring leaders and frankly also to old horses like me. DP

From 5:00 this morning until about 7:00 I read your book. It is absolutely awesome! You should be very proud of this book. I'm going to encourage some people in my organization to read this book so I might want to purchase some. Are they available? CC

Taylor read your book from cover to cover the moment he got home, and I completed it last night thanks to your generosity. Your book should be required reading for each boy!! I have attended many motivational and leadership conferences through my years but your book encapsulates everything one would ever need to build or improve themselves and more importantly others. Thank you sincerely from our hearts. IH

TABLE OF CONTENTS

PREFACE

THE MATERIAL FOR THIS BOOK HAS BEEN COLLECTED OVER MORE THAN 30 YEARS AND HAS BEEN ASSIMILATED TO PROVIDE ADVICE AND COUNSEL FOR YOUNG LEADERS WHO WISH TO EXERCISE THE ART AND SCIENCE OF LEADERSHIP IN THE MILITARY, BUSINESS, GOVERNMENT, HEALTH INDUSTRY, AND SCHOOLS. I believe the contents are especially appropriate for cadets and alumni of military schools and young officers as an aid to their development as America's future leaders. Some of the material emanates from my reading, but other portions relate directly to the many leadership mistakes that I have made as an officer in the United States Marine Corps and in higher education. I have sought to include pearls of wisdom that are memorable—pearls that will be there when the leader must make a decision and when the information for doing so is gray or non-existent. I offer these insights in hopes that young leaders can learn vicariously, eliminating the mistakes that I made in my "trial and error" way of leading.

In his book entitled *Integrity*, Henry Cloud wrote that one's personal makeup is germane to the results of the task at hand. The results, or **wake,** as Cloud described it, have two parts–mission results and relationships. After a few years in an organization, one establishes a record of achievement and a record of personal dealings that make up the **wake**. Either dimension of the wake can be positive or negative. "The wake doesn't lie and it doesn't care about excuses," according to Cloud. Cloud's writing struck a nerve with me as I have realized for some time that as a Marine officer I could be too mission-oriented, completely overlooking the fact that there was an empathetic component to leadership.

Leadership is not an end state but a process. As the President of Riverside Military Academy, I am still learning and still making mistakes. Hopefully, these mistakes are not as egregious as those made in my earlier years. As you pursue your education and subsequent leadership opportunities, I encourage you to continue your leadership studies and always remember–You Can, You Will, You Must Succeed.

James H. Benson
Colonel of Marines–Retired

INTRODUCTION

"The secret of all victory lies in the organization of the non-obvious."
O SWALD S PENGLER

"Winners are those people who make a habit of doing the things losers are uncomfortable doing."
E D F OREMAN

"Ever notice that people never say, 'It's only a game' when they are winning?"
I VERN B ALL

"Good leaders are intense; real good leaders are passionate; but great leaders are predators when it comes to winning on the battlefield, the gridiron, or in the workplace."
J IM B ENSON

T HROUGH THE YEARS, I HAVE BEEN INTRIGUED BY THE CONSISTENT SUCCESS OF SOME LEADERS. Why are some people successful leaders within the organization while others, with superior intellect and academic credentials, are less successful or blatantly unsuccessful? Why are others quite successful in one position or assignment, but, when promoted, fail miserably? Why are there great assistant coaches in the college and professional athletic ranks who simply cannot win once they assume the role of head coach?

As a U.S. Marine Corps officer, I was in the unique position of observing the leadership products of our nation's colleges and universities for 26 years. I have led and observed second and first lieutenants from Harvard, Stanford, MIT, Ball State, Texas A&M, and the U.S. Naval Academy, to name a few. All I can conclude from this experience is that where a lieutenant went to college and what he majored in had no bearing whatsoever on his ability to lead men and women to greater levels of achievement. I can make judgments as to intellect and academic prowess based on university of record and major subject area; but there is no observable correlation with success in a leadership capacity. One correlation that I can make is, when an officer genuinely desires to lead a unit and takes full responsibility for its success or failure, he is generally successful.

Another characteristic, which is readily observable in successful lieutenants, was the ability to craft a solution to a problem and implement the solution. It appears that our colleges and universities do a fair job in the crafting solutions piece through problem-solving classes and case studies. *But no where do we teach them how to discern problems before they become major issues.* In my judgment, problem-finding may be as important as problem-solving, and it apparently involves a combination of insight, critical observation, common sense, and maybe an innate feeling in the gut of the leader.

Although not just about leadership per se, this book deals with the leader's number one resource—people. Some years ago when reading Mark McCormick's book entitled *What*

They Don't Teach at the Harvard Business School, I was taken with Mark's ability to get right down to the essence of success in the business world. He titled Section I, PEOPLE. And, quite frankly, that is what this book is about. It's about the science of motivation. How do some leaders get people to do the things that are essential to success?

I have come to the realization that leaders succeed with people–not with elaborate goals, objectives or strategies, but by finding good people, getting them in the right job, and then motivating them to perform close to their abilities. General U. S. Grant recorded in his memoirs, "few of my officers knew that I had never bothered to study tactics." It is true, a great tactician, Grant was not. But a man of vision and organization, he was, and undoubtedly, a leader who got the most out of his people.

I have found that successful leaders and managers tend to be generalists who possess the skills necessary to motivate and influence others towards superior levels of performance consistent with their abilities and on occasion, well beyond their perceived abilities. Yes, I say skills because these attributes can be learned. Otherwise, there would be no need for this book nor any of the hundreds on the subjects of leadership, managership, and motivation that fill the shelves of America's libraries and shopping center bookstores today.

Much of the narrative herein deals with personal experience and observations in over 26 years as an officer of the U.S. Marines, but I also call on experience, observations, and readings in the fields of business, academics, higher education, and athletics. The ideas and principles here are just as applicable to the small business entrepreneur, corporate

CEO, or Baptist minister as to the young U.S. Army lieutenant or high school basketball coach.

Much of today's literature on leadership and success is written by and in many cases for the academician. This book is anything but a magnum opus, but it contains practical information, which leaders can employ immediately in their quest for success on the gridiron of life. It is purposely less intellectual in approach, hopefully inspirational, and should be easily read, understood, and enjoyed by prospective leaders and managers at all levels who simply want to better their ability to lead their soldiers, workers, or players to higher levels of performance. Hence, it is especially for winners. For those who are already winners, they will be affirmed and hopefully their skills further honed. For those who are only part-time or sometime winners, they may see the error of their ways. For those satisfied with the status quo, they aren't going to read this book anyway.

SECTION 1

THE ROAD TO COMPREHENSION

"Success has no time for patience."
JIM BENSON

*"No one does medicine, does law, or does leadership–
one practices it."*
ANONYMOUS

I SHALL NOT BECOME DEEPLY EMBROILED IN DIFFERENTIATING BETWEEN LEADERSHIP AND MANAGEMENT NOR SUCCESS VIS-A-VIS WINNING. For purposes herein, leadership implies the handling of people, and management the handling of things. It is a given that leaders must also handle things, and managers also handle people, hence, it's a wash. Success and winning are virtually synonymous. Webster's dictionary describes success as "the attainment of wealth, favor and eminence, a favorable termination of a venture." Likewise, winning is defined as "the achievement of success in an effort or venture, to attain a desired goal or end state." Throughout this book, I shall refer to the winner as one who is successful on the gridiron of life–one who consistently achieves his or her (hereafter, the female pronoun will be omitted

5

for the sake of space and repetition, but everything herein is just as applicable to the female gender as to the male) desired end state, be it advancement up the corporate ladder, the college or university hierarchy, or the military chain of command.

Winning is a dynamic process. The variables (economy, available talent, education, opportunity, etc.) continually shift and the players must adjust accordingly. The measurement of success is a challenge. Most measure success in terms of wealth accrued. Conrad Hilton in his book, "Be My Guest," tells us that success is not measured by the accumulation of money. According to Hilton, "Too many rich men are failures and too many poor men masters of the art of living to make this the criterion. Mahatma Gandhi, one the most successful statesmen of our time, left, upon his death as his entire worldly estate: two rice bowls, one spoon, two pairs of sandals, his copy of the Bhagavad-Gita, his spectacles, and an old-fashioned watch. The yardstick for measuring success would seem to be not how much a man gets as how much he has to give away."

Ralph Waldo Emerson wrote, "To laugh often and much; to win the respect of intelligent persons and the affection of children; to earn the appreciation of honest critics and endure the betrayal of false friends; to appreciate beauty; to find the best in others; to leave the world a bit better, whether by a healthy child, a garden patch or a redeemed social condition; to know even one life has breathed easier because you have lived. This is to have succeeded."

There is individual success as previously described by Emerson, and there is success within the organization, which revolves around the skills of the leader. This book focuses on the successful leader and how his success manifests itself in victory within and for the organization. Nonetheless, much of what is essential to success in the organization is also compatible with individual success.

Adherence to the principles in this book or any book will not in itself guarantee victory within the organization. There are just too many variables. But adherence will help one avoid many of the pitfalls resulting from inexperience and naiveté. The wisdom herein is from the minds of many winners, and if consumed by the reader, will vicariously provide experience, which it might otherwise take years to acquire. If you read this book thoroughly, highlight portions that apply to your situation, then occasionally review the highlighted portions, over time, you will sway the pendulum towards victory. Meanwhile, you will be a happier person, perform in a more positive environment, appreciate your associates more, and move up the ladder to greater victories. And after all, isn't this what winning is all about?

SECTION 2

REAL LEADERS

"Leadership is the single most important organizational factor separating the winners and the also-rans."
DAVID COTTRELL

*"Obey your leaders and submit to their authority.
They keep watch over you as men who must give an account.
Obey them so that their work will be a joy,
not a burden, for that would be of no advantage to you."*
JAMES 1:1

*"The basis of leadership is the capacity to change the mindset,
the framework of another person."*
WARREN BENNIS

"Lead, and I will follow."
ALFRED, LORD TENNYSON

I HAVE ALWAYS BEEN MORE INTERESTED IN PEOPLE THAN IN THINGS, SO I GUESS I HAVE BECOME A STUDENT OF PEOPLE INSOMUCH AS I WANT TO KNOW EVERYTHING THERE IS TO MAKE THEM PERFORM NEAR THEIR POTENTIAL. In recent years, I have come to the conclusion that **real leaders are an endangered species**. What has become of the outspoken, emboldened, charismatic, competitive, and decisive leader who established superior standards of

8

excellence and performance and held his charges feet to the fire in the achievement of these standards? Yes, this is the same guy who inspired us all to levels of performance that we could never have envisioned and secured our complete loyalty to the organization, which he represented. Instead, it seems that we have developed politically correct do-gooders, who socialize their way up the ladder without challenging the status quo, offending any group, or risking failure whatsoever. They tolerate incompetence and marginal performance rather than risk the confrontation or perceived leadership failure necessary to fire the culprit. Woe be unto the leader who actually displays temper or emotion and "gets in the face" of a non-performer whose actions or lack thereof are affecting the accomplishments of the organization as a whole. According to James Stockdale, retired Vice Admiral and Congressional Medal of Honor Winner:

Glib, cerebral, detached people can get by in positions of authority until the pressure is on. But when the crunch comes, people cling to those they know they can trust—those who are not detached, but involved—those who have consciences, those who can repent, those who do not dodge unpleasantness. Such people can mete out punishment and look their charges in the eye as they do it. In difficult situations, the leader with the heart, not the bleeding heart, not the soft heart, but the Old Testament heart, the hard heart, comes into his own.

Real leaders are not prima donnas; albeit they may be arrogant, moody, nonconforming, dissenters who demand excellence and possess a low tolerance for mediocrity or idleness. They often have an extraordinary eye for detail and insist on loyalty and dedication from their people. Likewise, they are genuinely caring and loyal and are always looking to better the lot of their people. They can motivate with a disdaining look or comment. There is never a doubt as to what is expected. They do not fear controversy; in fact, they often relish it. Although respected, they are not necessarily popular. According to Texas Tech University basketball coach, Bobby Knight, "Popular people don't make particularly good leaders; decisive people with judgment who aren't afraid to tell other people who don't have such good judgment that their judgment isn't very good, make good leaders."

Effective leadership is the cornerstone of every organization including corporations, military units, Little League baseball teams, small town police forces, fast food restaurants, and small businesses. Hence, I am continually amazed at the naiveté of the owners of professional football, basketball, baseball, and hockey teams. Seldom does the acquisition of one player turn a loser into a winner. Yet owners continuously invest huge sums in the purchase and contract of one superstar and then skimp on the acquisition of a coach or manager whose leadership affects the performance of every player, thus affecting the entire image and profit-making ability of the team. George Steinbrenner, owner of the New York Yankees, and the late Charley Finley, owner of the Oakland A's, broke the code more than once with the hiring of the late Billy Martin. Brash, non-conforming, do-it-his-way Billy, was able to turn around the fortunes of virtually every team he managed. He was a leader and a winner by anyone's standards. Nonetheless, Billy's personal characteristics would

10

eventually lead to his demise, but he knew how to win. The prudent owner starts by hiring the best manager or coach he can get, regardless of the cost, one who can get the maximum out of the available talent, and then he procures those players who can fill the voids. True leaders are able to get average players to play above their perceived abilities. Hence, in following years they become trading material for players with greater talent who have not reached their potential while playing for lesser managers or coaches. Although it may seem unfair, it happens all the time, and the average player usually reverts to his average performance once disassociated from the real leader.

Leaders and managers often speak of the necessity of acquiring "the horses" to elevate the performance of the organization. The horses are generally viewed as the players or specialists. Not to me; the horses are the leaders! If a team or department is mediocre, it probably needs a shot in the arm. It needs someone who has the force of personality to raise the standards and demand adherence to them. On the selection of leaders, "you can put a mule in the Kentucky Derby, but you have to kick his fanny all the way around the track and even then you won't win the roses or get kissed by the pretty girl."

It seems that even our great military has succumbed to temptation to honor the politically astute rather than the warrior. Neither, U. S. Army Lieutenant General George Patton nor U. S. Marine Lieutenant General Lewis (Chesty) Puller would be General officers in today's military. Patton has been described as vain, insecure, brutal, and arrogant. Likewise, he could be sensitive and humble. He lived for recognition and approval. He was obsessed with success at any cost. Neither Patton nor Puller could survive the political correctness expectations existent in today's military, and I see the same indicators in the public and private sectors. "Boat-rockers" are not in demand. Many resist the need to break paradigms and initiate change. Instead, they seek new mentors in high positions, retain the status quo, avoid decisions that could be controversial, and position themselves for advancement.

Winners are looking for leaders who are risk-takers, but risk-takers with common sense. Real leaders generate action and thrive on achievement and not necessarily their own. The glory is seeing their people excel. They seek leaders who are intelligent, but not necessarily intellectual. They seek leaders who are relentless in their quest for success. They seek leaders with charisma who can motivate and inspire.

When Aeschines spoke, they said: "How well he speaks, what glorious words, what magnificent tones."

But when Demosthenes spoke, they shouted, "Let us march against Philip. Now."

SECTION 3

FEAR, COURAGE, AND WINNING

"Fear is that little dark room where negatives are developed."
MICHAEL PRITCHARD

"...the only thing we have to fear is fear itself."
FRANKLIN D. ROOSEVELT

*"I would define true courage to be a perfect sensibility
of the measure of danger, and a mental willingness to incur it."*
W. T. SHERMAN

"Courage is being scared to death but saddling up anyway."
ANONYMOUS

WE GENERALLY THINK OF PHYSICAL COURAGE AND BRAVERY WHEN WE
DISCUSS COURAGE. Many writings on courage and fear relate
to combat heroes. However, real courage manifests itself
more quietly when one takes a public position that does not
conform to the masses, when taking the harder right over
the easier wrong, when refusing to laugh at others' blunders, and when voicing one's conviction with passion when
the conviction will be counter to the desires of the boss.

Real leaders also demonstrate courage when they
accept risk and make the hard decisions that desert the

status quo. Giving responsibility and authority to subordinates is also courageous because of the increased risk of temporary failure. Nonetheless, the leader knows that subordinate growth and job satisfaction are worth the risk of temporary failure.

Physical courage relates to one's ability to overcome real and immediate fear. According to George S. Patton, Jr., "All men are frightened. The more intelligent they are, the more they are frightened. The courageous man is the man who forces himself, in spite of his fear, to carry on. Discipline, pride, self-respect, self confidence, and love of glory are attributes, which will make a man courageous even when he is afraid." There is truth in General Patton's statement, but he omitted what may be the greatest incentive to overcome fear and that is the internal pressure to not let down one's friends and comrades.

Preparation that leads to poise and confidence overcomes fear. I know fear first hand. Twice, I was caught in an open field with no cover or concealment on the receiving end of a daylight ambush. In both cases, I was a platoon commander in Quang Nam Province in Viet Nam. In each case, I was initially terrified, but as a leader I put on my "mean game face" and took on the appearance of controlled rage, profanely shouting orders and in one instance leading the assault through the ambush. I believe I learned controlled rage on the football field. As a quarterback, I could be quite an actor in the huddle, as I admonished linemen for missing their blocks and challenging backs to get the yard needed for a first down or a touchdown.

In Viet Nam, I required daylight patrols and night ambushes to wear camouflage paint (war paint), because I

14

wanted the men to look mean. I wanted the Viet Cong to fear us. It served another purpose. It made the men feel prepared and ready, and they were good. The only problem with the paint was that the stuff didn't want to come off after the patrol, so the troops didn't like to wear it.

One of the most courageous men I served with in Viet Nam was a Hospital Corpsman (HM3) named "Doc" Hargett. As I recall, "Doc" was a high school football player with a strong sense of personal values. Although he stepped up often, I will never forget a morning along the Son Cu De River. I had led a platoon-sized patrol through a hamlet inhabited by Viet Cong at dusk one evening. We dropped off a two man sniper team with a third Marine carrying a PRC-25 radio. The intent was that the sniper team would occupy a hide site until first light the next morning. Just before daylight the snipers would maneuver to a vantage point and destroy Viet Cong soldiers when they attempted to exit the hamlet. They would frequently sneak into the hamlet at night to see their families and leave at or near first light the next morning to occupy their underground hiding place during daylight hours. After dropping off the snipers, the platoon-sized patrol moved a couple of kilometers away and set up a perimeter defensive position for the night. However, around 6:00 AM the next morning, the platoon received a radio call that the snipers were engaged in a fire fight. We immediately saddled up and returned to the hamlet on a dead run. Upon arrival at the hide site, we found the radio operator who said the firing had ceased about the time of his initial radio call. He feared that the snipers were dead or captured. The two snipers had apparently occupied a vantage point on a small rise about a football field's distance from the hide site. It was clear to me that someone had to go up and find the snipers. I wanted the platoon to move to a position perpendicular to the route of movement to the snipers' assumed position. As I explained the plan and looked into the eyes of the squad leaders for volunteers, all began to look at their boots except "Doc" Hargett who said, "I'll go." It was one of those times that I knew I had to lead, so I told the platoon sergeant to move the platoon to the designated position and to set up a base of fire to cover the movement of "Doc" and me as we crawled through the seven foot elephant grass to search for the snipers. After arranging for the proper visual signals, "Doc" and I began our crawl forward. The sun was up and the climate was steamy. We reached the knoll without contact and found the snipers dead—they had been shot in the head and neck dozens of times. "Doc" immediately picked up the bigger of the two snipers, and I took the smaller one. Nonetheless, he was dead weight and was so shot up that his cranial bones rattled and his blood ran down the back of my clothes under my shirt and flak jacket. This coupled with the heat caused me to become light headed and half way down the hill I fell with the body shifting forward and forcing my face into the mud. I felt as if I was going to pass out and had no strength. Somehow while still carrying the other body, "Doc" Hargett helped me to my feet while adjusting my load. We gathered ourselves for a moment, and "Doc" said, "Come on sir, let's get the hell out of here." We then proceeded back to the platoon without further incident. I have never forgotten that incident. I have no idea where "Doc" got the strength to get me up and going while still carrying his load, which was greater than mine. I know that from that point on I was barely functioning physically and although I was the lieutenant and "Doc" was a Hospital Corpsman, he was the leader, and I was the follower for those minutes.

To summarize this section, courage is mental and physical. One does not have to be a soldier, Marine, fireman, or law enforcement officer to show courage. It is needed in the corporate board room, in schools, churches, and certainly in government.

SECTION 4

INTEGER

"Talent is a gift, but character is a choice."
JOHN MAXWELL

*"There is harmony and inner peace to be found
in following a moral compass
that points in the same direction, regardless of fashion or trend."*
TED KOPPEL

*"By themselves, character and integrity
do not accomplish anything.
But their absence faults everything else."*
PETER DRUCKER

"Integrity is the spotlight into the leader's soul."
GENERAL CHARLES C. KRULAK, USMC (RET)

ACCORDING TO FORMER U.S. MARINE CORPS COMMANDANT, GENERAL CHARLES KRULAK, AS ROMAN SOCIETY DETERIORATED, TENSION DEVELOPED BETWEEN THE LEGIONNAIRES AND PRAETORIANS, WHO WERE THE IMPERIAL BODYGUARDS. As the well-connected praetorians ascended into favor, they would strike their breastplates and shout, "Hail Caesar." To emphasize their differences from the praetorians, the legionnaires would strike their armor and shout, "Integer," which means undiminished, complete,

18

perfect. The legionnaire was emphasizing his character in contrast to the immoral conduct of the praetorians.

The absence of integrity is observed in many forms. Stephen Carter, author of *Integrity*, wrote that, "An integrity crisis affects U. S. society." Carter found school administrators who confuse their educational mission with winning in athletics, journalists who write their stories without the facts, schools with inflated grades and low academic standards, police corruption, and more.

Michael Josephson, president and founder of the Josephson Institute on Ethics writes that, "We're in a state of moral malaise." He claims that U. S. citizens are not proud of themselves, their government, or their leaders ostensibly due to the demise of our societal integrity.

A Gallup poll of American executives discovered that 80 percent drive while under the influence, 35 percent cheat on their taxes, 75 percent use company supplies for non-company business, and 78 percent make personal, long-distance phone calls on the company telephones.

My experience has been that dishonesty is most likely to manifest itself in deceit. Thus, I find deceit the most hideous form of dishonesty, because its intent is to deceive. Whether its form is exaggeration of the good to cover the bad, the use of guile and cunning to promote oneself above others, or the cover up of error and failure, deceit is a cardinal sin that is next to impossible to forgive.

I appreciate Denis Waitley's story of how the surgeon tested the integrity of a new nurse in *Empires of the Mind*.

"It was the surgical nurse's first day on the medical team. She was responsible for ensuring that all the instruments and materials were accounted for before the operation was completed. As the surgeon prepared to sew up the incision, she noticed that the surgeon had removed only 11 sponges from the patient, and she was positive they had used 12.

– No, I removed them all, the doctor told her. We'll close up now.

– No, insisted the nurse, we used 12 sponges.

– I'll take the responsibility, said the surgeon. I'm ready to close up now.

– You can't do that sir, said the nurse. Think of the patient. The surgeon lifted his foot, revealing the 12th sponge hidden beneath his shoe. You'll do just fine in this or any other hospital, he said with a smile."

Retired Marine Brigadier General Tom Draude stated, "Marines don't measure what they say against the political correctness yardstick. We deal in truth, in the lack of guile, and that sometimes will be perceived as insensitive." No one can claim perfect integrity, and all of the military services have experienced moral failure within their ranks. But from my 26 years of experience as a Marine officer, there is a distain for dishonesty within the Marines that exceeds any organization in which I have been associated.

In his book, *Over the Top*, Zig Zigler encouraged leaders to conduct their lives as if, "The mike is open and the camera is on (us)." Whether we are writing a report, preparing our taxes, explaining an incident where we might have a degree of culpability, or filing an insurance claim, leaders must resist the temptation to deceive. I am convinced that everyday actions and decisions at home and at work, not made from a values-based foundation, cause problems with stability within the family, workplace, and unit.

Integer!

SECTION 5

DISHONESTY AND DISLOYALTY DESERVE NO SECOND CHANCE

"It isn't the people you fire who make your life miserable,
it's the people you don't."
HARVEY MACKAY

"Suffer long for mediocre but loyal Huns.
Suffer not for competent but disloyal Huns."
ATTILA THE HUN

OF THE FIVE MOST SIGNIFICANT ON-THE-JOB MISTAKES THAT I HAVE MADE DURING 26 YEARS OF SERVICE IN THE U.S. MARINE CORPS AND SUBSEQUENT YEARS AS A SENIOR COLLEGE ADMINISTRATOR, FOUR INVOLVE THE FAILURE TO FIRE SUBORDINATES WHEN MY INSTINCTS TOLD ME TO DO SO.

The three most notable reasons for firing are dishonesty, disloyalty, and apathy on the job. The first two I will not tolerate for a moment. The third I can work with – for a while. It is a challenge to try to motivate an apathetic worker. Incompetence is certainly reason for dismissal, but if an incompetent employee gives 100%, I usually work hard at finding a place where he can contribute.

Undoubtedly, one of the toughest and most important decisions facing a leader or manager is when to fire a worker or subordinate leader or manager. The positive or negative after effects will invariably ricochet throughout the organization. Harold Geneen, the late ITT Chief Executive Officer, said, "this decision is the most acute test of the leadership of an organization." The rank and file pass judgment on what the boss did and how it was done. They respect the leader who makes the tough decision but expect compassion in the method in which it is done.

In most instances, firing an employee should be a deliberate and contemplated endeavor. It should seldom be on the spur of the moment (except in isolated cases of dishonesty and disloyalty) and generally should follow well-planned and rehearsed counseling. Counseling should be face-to-face and specific in nature. Faint praise and counseling by innuendo will not suffice. The worker must be told of his shortcomings, offered a plan for improvement, and given a fair amount of time to put the new regimen into practice. Follow-up sessions are appropriate for those who make a concerted effort to improve but still are not quite achieving the goal.

Dishonesty and disloyalty deserve no second chance. But it is important that the leader/manager make that fact known up front. Dishonesty and disloyalty are often hard to detect. Frequently, we suspect one or the other, but proof eludes us. But once either is assured, the winner will act and act swiftly.

Steven Brown advises, "When you have determined in your mind that the person is destined to failure, terminate him or transfer him to a position for which he is better suited. Don't keep him around to die a slow death and suffer the agony of being undermined by you. If the other party becomes equally involved in the fault-finding, one of you had better dust off the luggage, because no one building will be large enough for both of you."

In summary:

- Fire with compassion, but fire when necessary. Trust your instincts—when it's time, it's time. Try to let the employee being dismissed save face if at all possible. But in some cases, it may be appropriate to fire quickly and with "measured malice." The winner realizes that a backlash may occur within the unit if he appears ruthless and cold in carrying out a dismissal.
- Resist the temptation to fire on the spur of the moment without warning or counseling, except in extreme cases.
- Never suffer dishonesty or disloyalty.

In his first book, "Creating Magic," Lee Cockerell wrote that, "a leader's job is to do what has to be done, when it has to be done, in the way it has to be done, whether you like it or not, and whether they like it or not."

SECTION 6

POWER AND AUTHORITY—
THE GOOD, THE BAD, AND THE EVIL

"Power is an aphrodisiac."
HENRY KISSINGER

*"Nearly all men can stand adversity,
but if you want to test a man's character,
give him power."*
ABRAHAM LINCOLN, 1809–1865

*"The fundamental concept in social science is power,
in the same sense in which energy
is the fundamental concept in physics."*
BERTRARD RUSSELL

"Power tends to corrupt, and absolute power corrupts absolutely."
LORD ACTON

THE MENTION OF THE WORD POWER CONNOTATES AN UNEASY FEEL-
ING AMONG MANY. We tend to envision power as akin to the
domineering, authority figure. But in reality, power is the
essence of persuasion without force; it is the winner's ability to inspire others to achieve.

Of course, throughout history, power has been abused
to the extent many fear it. The new leader's use of power

24

will be closely observed and evaluated by the team, unit or workforce. The experienced leader will expect as much and will be extremely judicious in the use of recently acquired power, especially in the early days and weeks after assuming a position of authority.

Numerous psychological studies report that the need to influence others through power is a greater need among winners than the need to be liked or even to achieve personally. Real leaders use power surreptitiously and in a way that preserves a harmonious balance.

Power and authority are virtually synonymous terms. But power can have a sinister connotation. Authority is more subtle. How leaders use power is directly related to the success they are able to bring about.

It is known that power has the capacity to corrupt. History is replete with individuals whose egos enlarged dramatically with the assumption of significant authority over others. Often, power is viewed as the culprit when seemingly good people become engaged in unethical activities. Some in power come to believe that they are above the company regulations and even the law. We have all observed how the assumption of a position of power can cloud the judgment of the leader. Thomas Babington summed it up well, "The highest proof of virtue is to possess boundless power without abusing it."

Power placed in the hands of the non-leader can be fraught with danger. He may resort to coercive power that uses threats and sanctions to achieve compliance and obedience. John Gardner, in his fine book, *On Leadership*, wrote that, "…we must not confuse leadership with power. Leaders always have some measure of power rooted in their capacity to persuade, but many people with power are without leadership gifts. Their power derives from money, or from the capacity to inflict harm, or from control of some piece of institutional machinery."

In summary, the nature of leadership relates to how the leader uses the power associated with his organizational authority. Except in the exigencies of combat, police work, and firefighting, absolute and immediate response to direction from the leader is rarely prescribed. In other situations, a more subtle, deliberate, and persuasive use of power is appropriate.

SECTION 7

TRUST, CONFIDENCE, AND PREDICTABILITY

"I trust everyone but still cut the cards."
FINLEY PETER DUNNE

*"Few things help an individual more than to place responsibility
upon him and to let him know that you trust him."*
BOOKER T. WASHINGTON, 1896–1915

*"What upsets me is not that you lied to me,
but that from now on I can no longer believe you."*
FRIEDRICK W. NIETZSCHE, 1844–1900

"It is better to be defeated on principle than to win on lies."
ARTHUR CALDWELL

LEADERS TEND TO RECRUIT AND RETAIN PEOPLE WHO ARE PREDICTABLE
AND TRUSTWORTHY. We see it time and again as leaders (corporate heads, civilian government officials, and military officers) take key staff members with them when they move
to new positions. Many times the hiring and transfer of
staff is not necessarily due to competence but to predict-
ability and dependability. Frequently, I have seen simply
adequate but trustworthy performers moved along by

leaders when, in fact, better talent was already existent within the new organization.

Leaders tend to adopt and promote people in whom they have developed trust and confidence. Trust and confidence are earned by people who are forthright and honest. Early on, the leader is evaluating everything he is told by a new employee. He wants to know–is this guy believable? Does he color the truth? Does he build himself up by sniping at his peers? Does he magnify his own worth by boasting? Does this guy exaggerate the good and play down the bad? When I ask for his opinion or recommendation, does he give me his unambiguous, unequivocal yes or no, concur or non-concur, or agree or disagree, and why? I don't want it sugar-coated, and I don't have time to figure out what he means. According to Robert Ringer, "Another common form of lying that most people don't normally think of as lying is exaggeration. Nothing makes me lose confidence in a person more quickly than to discover that he inflates his facts or feats."

Conrad Hilton wrote that, "Once you start it, there's no place that deception can stop–and of course it has to start with self-deception, even if it's only the self-deception of believing we can get away with it. True, sometimes we are not discovered. But all of modern psychology and psychiatry is based on the belief that our self-deceptions drive things into our subconscious where they make all kinds of trouble."

Alibis, excuses, and passing the blame are bane to trust and confidence. When winners mess up, they fess up. They realize that everyone messes up sometimes so their competence is not in question (of course, repeated ill-advised and/or foolish mistakes will risk one's reputation for competence), but failure to own up puts one's credibility at risk.

In his book, *13 Fatal Errors Managers Make and How You Can Avoid Them,* Steven Brown describes 'Internalists' as performance-oriented people and those who hide behind alibis and excuses as 'Externalists.' He claims that "people fail in direct proportion to their willingness to accept socially acceptable excuses for failure." According to Brown, Externalists position themselves as victims while Internalists take the hand they are dealt and play it to the hilt.

To nurture trust and confidence in oneself, the winner:

- Quickly owns up to errors, blunders and lapses (after all, we all make errors).
- Personally tells the boss of blunders before someone else does.
- Accepts full blame and avoids alibis (even if partial blame belongs elsewhere).
- If at fault, states accurately or slightly overstates the damage. Never fear, someone else will explain the real damage, and you will be vindicated while your credibility actually grows.

Winners are always searching for other winners. They are looking for people who are believable all the time. Robert Ringer tells us that, "All lies have one thing in common, and that's the price you pay when you're caught. And make no mistake about it, sooner or later you will be caught, which results in the most difficult of all losses to recoup – loss of credibility."

SECTION 8

UNIT MORALE – THE PREDOMINANT CHARACTERISTIC OF SUCCESSFUL ORGANIZATIONS

"Morale is the lifeblood of any team."
PAT RILEY

*"The failure to understand people
is the devastation of western management."*
W. EDWARDS DEMING

MORALE IS THE OXYGEN OF THE ORGANIZATION! Organizational morale, at any point in time, is directly proportional to the productivity of that organization. We have all seen organizations and teams floundering week after week and then suddenly as a result of some stimulus that dramatically enhances organizational morale, do a complete turnabout, accelerating productivity exponentially. Sometimes the stimulus is a change in leadership, a change in leadership technique, the acquisition of another team member who is able to generate enthusiasm, or simply a change in the environment or challenge.

For decades, winners have recognized the importance of morale in the development of winning organizations. Pat Riley says, "Morale is the lifeblood of any team." Napoleon is to have stated, "Morale is to numbers as three is to one." That statement implies that morale is a significant success multiplier to the organization.

It's easy to build a case for the importance of organizational morale. However, once one recognizes its importance, it is hard to comprehend why our schools, colleges, and universities fail to seek it. It seems that many educators would rather wallow in theory than in the science of motivation. So we continue to put our future leaders on the streets without the slightest perception of how to motivate their primary resource—people. According to Admiral David Farragut in a letter to his son in 1864, "Remember also that one of the requisite studies for an officer is man. Where your analytical geometry will serve you once, a knowledge of men will serve you daily." Harold Gineen put it succinctly, "...I do not think business schools are wrong in teaching what they do, but I do think their emphasis is lopsided. Too much attention is being paid in those schools to the mechanics and not enough to the emotional values of good business management." And, finally, to drive the point home one more time, W. Edwards Deming stated, "The failure to understand people is the devastation of western management."

Winners are students of the science of motivation. They read, digest, and understand the practical guidance offered by Peter Drucker, Warren Bennis, Mike McCormick, Norman Vincent Peale and yes, Pat Riley, Bill Walsh, and Mike Krzyzewski from the world of athletics. Whether we are talking about the secrets of George

Patton, Harry Truman, or Harold Mackay – the goal is the same, the development of winners through motivation.

Almost daily, I observe the failure of leaders to understand the ways and means of generating morale within the organization. Some years ago after observing my son's high school basketball team absorb another sound beating, the coach commented on the price they would pay in Monday's practice. In other words, the coach's motivation technique was to threaten and punish the team such that they would play harder next time. Occasionally, some players do need this type of motivator as a wake-up call. In this particular case and in many cases, the kids had played their hearts out and already felt punished enduring the loss itself. I submit that motivation techniques such as the above are usually counterproductive, affect player enthusiasm, and ultimately contribute to further losses. We've all observed techniques such as these in the work place, the classroom, and, unfortunately, on the Little League diamond. Often accompanying this technique are inflammatory remarks regarding the team or players' intestinal fortitude. This further denigrates the players' enthusiasm, nurturing resentment, distraction, and loss of focus. And, all so often in the case of youth athletics, a loss of the desire to ever participate in organized athletics again.

In all but the rarest of losses, leaders must accept their share of the blame and rally the team around the lessons learned and the next opportunity to win. Winners do not dwell on losses. They realize that the goal is to get morale as high as possible as quickly as possible. Several years ago, after observing the proud Duke University basketball team suffer a shellacking at home at the hands of the University of Virginia, I listened to Coach Krzyzewski in his post-game wrap up on AM radio. It was clear to me how Duke had won back-to-back national championships. Thirty minutes after the game, Coach Krzyzewski was already accepting blame for the loss, putting the team's mind at ease as to blame, and preparing to tackle the following week on a positive note. There was no scapegoat, no threats, only positive feedback. And as one would expect, they bounced back the following week with a crucial victory.

In the world of athletics and in the military, I have frequently heard the old adage about hard work and discipline being the keys to success. There is certainly some truth to this adage. However, I believe that dogmatic adherence to this maxim, particularly by young inexperienced leaders, has done more damage to organizational morale and hence, success, than any maxim I can recall. **The problem is that inexperienced and unlearned leaders can't discern when hard work and discipline turn into overwork and over-zealous discipline.** Overwork and over-zealous discipline destroy enthusiasm, create dissension, and cause serious deterioration of performance. Show me a coach or military leader who boasts about how hard his practices or training exercises are and I'll show you a coach or military leader who rarely has a record of success worth boasting about. The winner recognizes the limits of hard work and discipline and is able to achieve the training or work goals by challenging the team or work force without destroying the morale necessary to achieve success.

While on the subject of hard work and discipline, I want to tackle an associated error committed continuously in the field of athletics and the military by supposedly trained leaders attempting to maximize the performance of their players or soldiers. Through the years it has become crystal clear to me that over-training and conditioning are more damaging to unit performance than under-conditioning. In an under-conditioned unit, the players or soldiers may tire more quickly, but in an over-conditioned team, not only are the bodily reflexes sluggish, but the body is also susceptible to injury. Furthermore, unit attitude, morale, and enthusiasm are low before the event even begins! According to Bill Walsh when he coached the 49ers, "We never scheduled more than two hard workouts in a row, because I wanted to make sure players did not become so weary that they were unduly vulnerable to muscle pulls, or that their only concern in practice was to simply survive. It's vitally important that players or soldiers take the field to learn something rather than to have only their courage tested. This approach should be reflected all the way down to the Pop Warner level. There are only so many times when a coach (or military leader) should test an individual's courage or willingness to totally sacrifice."

I once read an interview that a sportswriter conducted with Greg Maddux, the superb Atlanta Braves and Chicago Cubs pitcher and Cy Young Award winner. Maddux relayed how he felt tired and worn out all the time during the season. When asked how he counteracted this, he replied, "I don't do anything. I rest – especially in the last two months of the season. I'm not worried about being in shape, because I am in shape. I'm not worried about missing a running day. If my legs are shot, I won't run. I'm not going to go out there and feel tired and then run myself into the ground and get even more tired. I'll take the day off. I'll give my body a day to come back on its own."

In many of the major blowouts in college and professional athletics, particularly in big games such as the Super Bowl when the tendency is to over-prepare, I believe the culprit is over-training. You can sense it in the lack of quickness (a telltale sign of over-training), mental lapses, and lack of genuine enthusiasm in the losing team. There is simply no other reason why teams with superb credentials can get so badly beaten. By the same token, I believe that many of the major upsets are accomplished by properly trained teams with fresh legs, mental sharpness, and enhanced enthusiasm against superior teams that have been over-trained and thereby, sacrificed their quickness, mental sharpness, and enthusiasm. Winners understand and practice common sense and some restraint in training their units. They know that failure to monitor training exercises or practices can undermine a unit's physical abilities and morale.

I am so convinced that morale is a major efficiency and capability multiplier that I believe it must be planned. **But who ever heard of a morale planning meeting?** I believe there are times when morale meetings are in order. The winner recognizes the **danger signals** of deteriorating morale. He is always on the alert for unusual absenteeism, observed boredom, idle standing around, lack of enthusiasm, obvious reluctance to speak or converse with leadership/ management, gossip and rumors, or a downright sultry attitude. The appearance of these traits in any number is a sure sign of deteriorating morale and calls for a meeting with subordinate leaders and maybe even the work force as a whole. Whatever the method, the problem has to be tackled head-on and immediately.

Winners sense the climate of the organization by getting out and talking to the unit or team members. According to former Brigadier General and author S.L.A. Marshall, "a common fault among young officers during World War II was to approach the troops with an attitude of condescension, intellectual separation and priggishness." I see this very trait today especially among young leaders educated at some of our more noted universities. Invariably, this lack of communication and failure to spot the danger signals cited earlier manifests itself in the morale and attitude of the unit. Moreover, once the problems begin to surface, the often-young leader begins to search for the scapegoat or he criticizes the unit members. On the contrary, the winner, upon observing the danger signals, asks himself the question, **"What am I doing wrong and how can I fix it?"**

I believe there exists a number of axioms, which are consistent with high morale in any organization:

- Individual morale is key to organizational or unit morale
- The actions of the leader are a primary ingredient of high or low morale
- Units with high morale are significantly more successful than organizations with low morale, and
- Organizations with **caring leaders** tend to exemplify the qualities of success much more frequently than those with leaders who are totally goal-focused.

Peters and Waterman wrote that excellent companies are people-oriented. Caring is a part of the institutional culture. In "lip service" companies, management still talks to people, but the substance is not there. Caring executives do everything possible before laying off workers. Their companies stand out as a result of their intense and persuasive concern for their work force. It is not hard to single out the leaders who sincerely care about the worker. They can be found out in the plant conversing, in the warehouse asking questions, and consistently searching for ways to better the lot of the worker. Whenever I think of the caring leader, I am reminded of the passage in Donald Hankey's *The Beloved Captain* when he described how the Captain cared for his men after the foot march:

We all knew instinctively that he was our superior – a man of finer fiber than ourselves, a 'toff' in his own right. I suppose that was why he could be so humble without loss of dignity. For he was humble too, if that is the right word, and I think it is. No trouble of ours was too small for him to attend to. When we started marches, for instance, and our feet were blistered and sore, as they often were at first, you would have thought that they were his own feet from the trouble he took. Of course, after the march, there was always an inspection of feet. That is the routine. But with him, it was no mere routine. He came into our room, and, if anyone had a sore foot, he would kneel down on the floor and look at it as carefully as if he had been a doctor. Then he would prescribe, and the remedies were ready at hand, being borne by a sergeant. If a blister had to be lanced, he would very likely lance it himself there and then, so as to make sure it was done with a clean needle and that no dirt was allowed to get in. There was no affection about this, no striving after effect. It was simply that he felt that our feet were pretty important, and that he knew that we were pretty careless. So he thought it best at the start to see to the matter himself. Nevertheless, there was, in our eyes, something almost

religious about this care for our feet. It seemed to have a touch of
Christ about it, and we loved and honored him the more.

It has been said that tact is the lubricating oil of human
relations. I suspect it has a significant effect on the morale
of an organization also. The real leader is thoughtful in his
approach to correction. He is careful in how he offers suggestions to the unit members such that they come across
with the desired effect.

It seems to me that the following actions on the part
of the leader lubricate the relationship between the leader
and the unit and have a significant impact on the morale
of the organization:

- Verbal compliments
- Reprimand judiciously, in private, to permit the subject
  to 'save face'
- Put the worker first; let him know that you think that
  he deserves the best pay and working conditions that
  the organization can afford to provide. Never pass up
  an opportunity to improve the lot of the worker.
- Better never to make a promise than to break one
- Remove the minor irritants (lack of paper products in
  the bathrooms, inconvenient parking, standing in line,
  insufficient breaks or time for lunch, unserviceable fur-
  niture or equipment, etc.), and
- Avoid ridicule and cajoling at all costs

There will always be those in the work force, the military,
and the athletic business who believe ridicule and cajoling
will motivate people to higher levels of performance. One
thing the winner knows for certain, if a team lacks drive,

enthusiasm, and the desire to excel, ridicule and cajoling will not give it to them.

In my judgment, one of the finest books on human relations ever written, was *How to Win Friends and Influence People* by Dale Carnegie. Carnegie says, "any fool can criticize, condemn, and complain – and most folks do." The leader's dilemma is how does he point out errors and shortfalls, particularly when they are repeated, without causing resentment, ill will, and morale deterioration. The winner does it by tactfully providing constructive criticism and convincing the unit that he sincerely cares about the welfare and upward mobility of the individual.

In conclusion, on what may be the most important section in this book, let me say that the morale of the unit or team is the essence of success, and I am reminded of a story told by a Baptist minister some years ago. According to the pastor, a Mennonite farmer explained that he had a horse that could pull 4500 pounds and another that could pull 4700 pounds, but together they pulled 12,000 pounds. This says much for the synergism of the team. Rudyard Kipling said it best in this great verse from his *Second Jungle Book*:

"Now this is the law of the Jungle – as old and as true as the sky;
And the Wolf that shall keep it may prosper, but the Wolf that shall break it must die.
As the creeper that girdles the tree-trunk, the law runneth forward and back;
For the strength of the Pack is the Wolf, and the strength of the Wolf is the Pack."

SECTION 9

SHAPING ATTITUDES

"There is real magic in enthusiasm.
It spells the difference between mediocrity and accomplishment."
NORMAN VINCENT PEALE

"Productivity increases
as managers increasingly understand the human factor
and effectively deal with the attitudes, fears, motivational blocks,
and the phantoms that lurk within the minds of people."
STEVEN BROWN

ACCORDING TO FORMER U. S. MARINE AND AUTHOR WILLIAM MANCHESTER, "I CAN DENOUNCE THE MARINE CORPS AND I FREQUENTLY HAVE. But so can lovers quarrel, and to those who have fought in it, the Corps is like the memory of an old affair, tinged with sadness and bitterness, yet with the first enchantment lingering. It is a mystique, wholly irrational; and right or wrong, a legion of men bred to logic will lay down their lives for its intangible honor tomorrow."

I know of no organization in western civilization that so shapes the attitudes of its people like the U. S. Marine Corps. But even after 26 years in this extraordinary outfit, I am not sure myself how it is done. I suspect that it starts with the Marine drill instructor. No Marine ever forgets his drill instructor. The drill instructor manifests perfection in appearance, attitude, demeanor, and competence. He or she becomes the role model. But it doesn't end there; the love and obedience to the principles of being a Marine seem to endure forever.

Who has ever observed a Marine in an airport terminal with his tie undone, his blouse off, or his shoes dirty? Marines are always erect in carriage, no nonsense in demeanor, and move about with confidence and poise. They represent the epitome of how leadership can shape the attitudes of the led.

Zig Zigler and others have written that the subconscious mind works to complete the picture painted by one's desires. In his book, *Think Like a Winner*, Walter Staples tells us that, "positive thinking does not allow the 10 percent that is not perfect in your life to influence and control 100 percent of your thinking and day-to-day existence." Staples continues to say that the subconscious mind will influence one's actions, demeanor, and behavior to fulfill one's self image. "The subconscious is always the obedient servant, the obliging slave to the conscious perception, and it is activated by mental pictures. But once it has received its instructions, it becomes the most powerful influence in your life," according to Staples. This helps explain the Marine mindset. Marines are what they are because they believe they are.

I am convinced that leaders can virtually will success and victory, but the mind must possess the right picture. Coach Joe Paterno wrote that, "when the mind, the body, and the entire nervous system are so focused on the desired end state, the forces can somehow compel the outcome." We see it in athletics where the near impossible upset occurs, and we see it in other organizations when the vision of the leader is so powerfully reinforced that the vision is realized. It is not about intelligence or intellect; it is much more than that. Some leaders have it and some do not.

Speaking of Coach Paterno, rarely has there been a leader and sports icon, whose life example has been admired for so long, fall from grace so quickly. As a Penn State alumnus, I am still in shock. Without seeing the hard evidence, it is hard for me to believe that Coach Paterno was as thoughtless, selfish, and lacking in wisdom to cover up the heinous sexual abuse that apparently occurred over the years.

SECTION 10

SELF-ESTEEM OF EMPLOYEES

"More than anything else, you and I seek self-esteem."
STEVEN BROWN

"My mother's kiss made me a painter."
BENJAMIN WEST **1738–1820**

SUCCESSFUL LEADERS NURTURE SELF-ESTEEM AMONG THEIR EMPLOYEES. Some positions, by their very nature, do not generate self-esteem, hence, individuals filling those positions sometimes punch the time clock, extend their breaks, and so forth and so on. They may be there for the paycheck. The successful leader will find ways to elevate the self-esteem of these people. Changing the name of the job, giving supervisory or quality control responsibilities based on performance or time on the job, and just plain verbal compliments may be helpful. Another way may have nothing to do with the job itself such as sponsorship of after work activities where employees can receive recognition other than on the job (heading the department bowling or softball team, successful participation in the company chess tournament, etc.). To maximize the employee's self-esteem after such endeavors, the leader must publicize the activity and the results. The leader is only limited by his imagination in these endeavors. Napoleon was exercising this principle when he acknowledged how much a man would do for a little piece of ribbon to wear upon his uniform.

Social scientists argue that empowerment of the workforce is consistent with worker self-esteem and progress. I hate the term, but I agree with the concept. Successful leaders are authorizing decisions at the lowest levels possible and accepting the inherent risks. They are calling on the ranks for ideas and then implementing them. This bottom-up input is being used in strategic development and decision-making. If one wants to call that empowerment – OK, but to me it is delegation of authority and common sense leadership.

SECTION 11

CREATE A WINNERS' CLIMATE

"Winning is not a sometime-thing here. It is an all-time thing."
Vince Lombardi

Organizational climate is a term in vogue in today's business schools. Command climate is a popular term in the military. In either case, climate refers to the work environment of an organization as perceived by the workers, and, yes, it is closely akin to morale. It can be found among the faculty of a school, the pilots of an airline, the coaching staff of a college, the sales force in a real estate office, or the ranks of a U. S. Marine rifle company. Many factors contribute to the organizational climate to include the work environment, the presence of cliques and favorites, the leadership style of a leader, the leader's genuine concern for his people, and the integrity of the unit's leadership.

Probably the easiest and quickest fix when a poor organizational climate exists is to improve the work environment. Few realize that "part of being good is looking good." Workers appreciate a professional environment, one that is clean, orderly and with a decor consistent with a quality product. Everyone wants to be proud of where they work. They genuinely like to bring their families and friends to their work place if it represents something they are proud to show off. I'm reminded of a downeast North Carolina high school where litter was strewn throughout the campus, grass and shrubs were never pruned, gymnasium bleachers were dirty, painting was long overdue, and the faculty appeared and acted indifferent towards the students. As one can imagine, student attitude was not conducive to learning. Attendance at school activities was demonstrative of the climate in that particular school. In my judgment, the organizational climate could have been improved significantly in one month of clean up, paint up, fix up.

The presence of cliques can have a serious effect on organizational climate. Cliques force the choosing of sides. Athletic coaches are very familiar with the dangers herein. Cliques can devastate a team. Even as a young 23-year-old high school football and baseball coach, I was ever observant for the formation of cliques. I even assigned lockers with the elimination of cliques in mind. The same was true of room assignments and vehicle assignments when playing on the road.

Vince Lombardi was ever fearful of the danger of cliques. "To minimize friction on the team, he deliberately made the players think of themselves as a unit, not as rookies and veterans, offense and defense, blacks and whites. Off the field the players congregated in different groups, with a variety of interests, but never formed cliques," according to Coach Lombardi.

As stated above, cliques have an immeasurable negative impact on the climate of an organization. The winner's goal is for everyone to feel like an integral part of the team and not be left out. Cliques do just the opposite. They imply that some are in the "in group" and some are not. The winner strives to foster unity of effort and a positive attitude among all players or workers. If everybody is comfortable in the organization and feels as if they are contributing, less time is spent fretting about position, and a wholesome unity of attitude is established.

The problem of cliques is exasperated if the leader himself is in a clique within the organization. In this case, resentment and petty jealousy are fostered and the winners' climate deteriorates into a losers' climate. This type of clique can often be found on high level organizational staffs. The winner is careful to keep even the appearance of such a relationship at bay.

In spite of the above, there is a tendency to have favorites due to similar interests, like personalities, personal appearance, etc., but winners wisely control or effectively hide such tendencies to preclude even the perception of favoritism because of the effect it can have on organizational climate. According to Coach Lombardi, "...he ceases to be a leader if he identifies too closely with the group. He must walk, as it were, a tightrope between the consent he must win and the control that he must exert."

Winners attack gossip and invective sniping head on. They refuse to participate in either, realizing that participation implies approval. Both are infectious and can seriously demean organizational climate and must be eliminated immediately when detected.

Winners avoid a faultfinding climate. By all means, the new student, player, soldier, or worker should not be initiated, trained, or oriented via verbal criticism or any form of punishment. The focus should be on progress, not failure.

Steven Brown wrote that, "Countless trainers have approached the learner with a machete in hand, chopped out the weaknesses, and then watched the person to death in perfection. The training arena has no place for ridicule, sarcasm, or negative critique." The exception to the above may be in the early stages of military recruit training when the trained and experienced drill instructor informs the recruit of his or her indulgent, self-centered lifestyle that is inimical to success in a military unit destined for combat.

In his work on managerial behavior, T. L. Daniel wrote that regardless of the name given to the leadership style, research indicates that a style that focuses on the mission and goals and provides an environment conducive to worker participation in all aspects of the organization is the style that facilitates a positive organizational climate.

A team, a faculty, a military unit, a corporate workforce, or a student body intuitively knows if there is a genuine care and concern for their welfare. Questions asked, things said and done, and body language in the aggregate demonstrate the attitude of the organization towards its people. Winners seize the opportunity to mingle with the workforce or team, ask the right questions, listen to the answers, and act where possible. They know how to exhibit care and understanding by visible actions that are for the benefit of the unit. Caring organizations invariably score high on organizational climate, and their level of achievement is consistent with this attitude.

Winners understand the techniques necessary to create a winner's climate. Additionally, they recognize the telltale signs of a declining organizational climate and are quick to tackle the causes.

SECTION 12

ORGANIZATIONAL ENVIRONMENT

"The winner is ever vigilant that the failure to frequently scan the rapidly changing environment is tantamount to defeat."
JIM BENSON

AN ORGANIZATION'S ENVIRONMENT REFERS TO THE EXTERNAL CONDITIONS THAT AFFECT ITS STRATEGY, MARKET, AND PROCESSES. The winner must continually adjust the sails to the wind. These constantly changing conditions are the focus of the winner. The actions of the Environmental Protection Agency (EPA) will have a major influence on everything from expansion of a business to the acquisition of materials necessary to run the business in America. A constantly changing technology can introduce a new competitor almost overnight. Changes in society's view of the work force with regard to minority rights, women in the workplace, and the provision of health care all influence the organizational environment. The company or corporate intelligence network is almost exclusively a covey of lawyers who are the "eyes and ears" of the organization in terms of its environment. The winner is ever vigilant that the failure to frequently scan the rapidly changing environment is tantamount to defeat in time.

SECTION 13

VISION

"Vision is the art of seeing things invisible."
JONATHAN SWIFT, **1667–1745**

"Where there is no vision, the people perish."
PROVERBS **29:18**

*"Vision is compelling, even compulsive,
which is both the problem and the power."*
HARRISON OWEN

"A man of vision plants trees under which he will never sit."
ANONYMOUS

SO MUCH HAS BEEN WRITTEN ON THE SUBJECT OF VISION AND STRATE-GIC INTENT IN RECENT YEARS THAT I HESITATE TO ADDRESS IT, BUT IT IS SO INTEGRAL TO WINNING THAT ITS OMISSION WOULD BE AN OBVIOUS VOID. I have seen it defined in various journals as mission, philosophy, purpose, and beliefs. I take exception with each of the definitions. The **mission** is what an organization does; it is the means. The **vision**, simply put, is the "desired end state" at some point in time. The philosophy and beliefs surrounding the vision are the guiding principles as to how the organization accomplishes its mission. The **purpose** of an organization is its reason for existence.

In the past two decades and to a large degree the result of worldwide recognition of the Deming theory of management, strategic planning and the resultant creation of an organizational vision have become vogue. However, visionary thinking has been existent in successful organizations for centuries. For the non-believers, read Wess Roberts' description of how, in 451 A.D., Attila the Hun took 700,000 barbarians, gave them a common purpose, discipline and esprit, and marched through eastern Europe at will in spite of "organized" resistance by seemingly superior forces.

Contrary to popular belief, all leaders are not visionary leaders. My theory is that leaders possess varying degrees of visionary abilities. Likewise, all are not conceptual thinkers. Nor are all even effective implementers in their own right. I see the visionary leader as one who clearly sees the end state of the organization at some point in time – maybe 1 year, 5 years, or 10 years. The conceptual thinker/planner is one who, when given the vision, sees and articulates the path to the end state. The implementer executes the plan. Ideally, the head of the organization (commander, president, or department head) would be a visionary who was previously successful as a planner with conceptual thinking skills. His operations officer would be a conceptual thinker who has also experienced previous success as an implementer. And, of course, the implementers would be the aggressive young lions capable of carrying out the operational plan devised by the operations officer.

Unfortunately, abilities and jobs are often mismatched. If the head of the organization is not a visionary, priorities continually change, reorganizations are frequent, and the organization flounders. If the operations officer is not a conceptual thinker, hence, cannot view the path to the vision; then the visionary head of the organization is soon ready for therapy. And, if the young implementers are really visionaries who prefer to sit and think about how things ought to be rather than getting their hands dirty making things happen, chaos is knocking at the door or already there.

The head of the organization must provide the vision. All have seen examples in the field of athletics where a great assistant coach fell from grace once given the responsibilities of head coach. As an assistant, he was given the vision, could visualize the path, and implement the process. However, as the head coach, he lacked the ability to visualize the end state and the components thereof. Hence, it was not long before he was again an assistant and probably once more, a successful one.

During the American Civil War, Lincoln had a great vision but until he appointed Grant as Commander in Chief, he was unable to find a General Officer who could comprehend his vision. The great leaders not only are visionary but they are able to articulate the vision to the unit and sell it as a recipe for success.

The great Chinese military strategist, Sun-tzu, demonstrated the point over 3,000 years ago that all men are not visionary when he said, "All men can see the tactics whereby I conquer, but what none can see is the strategy out of which great victory is evolved." The strategy, akin to the vision, was unknown to Sun-tzu's adversaries. According to Harrison Owen, "Visionaries are typically driven people. In the vernacular, they see things that others don't see, march to a different drummer, play by new rules."

I hate to dwell on the negative, but there are those who perceive themselves as visionaries and merchants of change yet have no strategic skills whatsoever. Perceived vision can be fatal as noted by Harrison Owen. I am always suspicious of those whose vision and reaction to every crisis or problem is reorganization. To compound the problem, these are usually the same folks who seldom follow through to effectively see to their vision or fully execute the change. They only create turbulence that invariably causes unexpected change within the organization that soon proves the reorganization a failure. Then the organization must endure the turbulence associated with reversing the change. Meanwhile, the rank and file wonder whether the drug urinalysis testing is aimed at the right group.

For those who possess visionary skills, they must be able to sell the vision to their constituents, demonstrate the competence to execute the actions necessary to implement the vision, and possess the devotion and stamina to see it through to completion.

SECTION 14

ORGANIZATIONAL VALUES

"Honesty is the first chapter of the book of wisdom."
THOMAS JEFFERSON

"Concentration is my motto –
first honesty, then industry, then concentration."
ANDREW CARNEGIE

"I hope I shall always possess firmness and virtue enough
to maintain what I consider the most enviable of all titles,
the character of an honest man."
GEORGE WASHINGTON

"Women and wine, game and deceit,
make the wealth small, and the wants great."
BEN FRANKLIN

SUCCESSFUL ORGANIZATIONS THAT ARE FOUNDED AND OPERATED AC-
CORDING TO A SET OF VALUES THAT ENCOURAGES HONESTY, MORALITY,
DIGNITY, INTEGRITY, AND TRUST INVARIABLY ARE SUCCESSFUL, RESPECTED,
AND JUSTIFIED. On the other hand, organizations that operate
and make decisions from a position of deceit and self-inter-
est, frequently experience marginal success and instability
within the work force. According to Robert Haas, CEO of
Levi-Strauss & Co, in an interview in the *Harvard Business*

Review, "we always talked about the hard stuff and the soft stuff. The soft stuff was the company's commitment to our work force. And the hard stuff was what really mattered, getting pants out the door. What we've learned is that the soft stuff and the hard stuff are becoming increasingly intertwined. A company's values – what it stands for, what its people believe in – are crucial to its competitive success. Indeed, values drive business."

People expect more of their leaders than they expect of themselves. They assume that leaders are men of integrity who base their daily decisions on a strong foundation of values. When they cease to believe this, problems surface with the stability of the workforce. Dishonesty, injustice, unfair business practices, and deceit are all contagious. If they exist at the top, they exist to some degree throughout the organization. When they exist throughout the organization, failure is imminent.

Winners realize that for a leader to be respected within the organization, he has to be respectable. Respect is earned by demonstrated competence, character, and integrity. Peter Drucker wrote that, "By themselves, character and integrity do not accomplish anything. But their absence faults everything else."

Small dishonesties can become habitual. I'm reminded of the 10-year-old boy who asked his father what the word "ethics" meant. The father said it had to do with telling the truth. For example, if I go to the bank to cash a check and the bank teller, by mistake, gives me $100 too much; I then have an ethical dilemma – Do I tell your mother that I have the extra $100 dollars or not?

Sir Walter Scott penned, "What a tangled web we weave, when first we practice to deceive." It is incredible what a chain reaction a single white lie can ignite. It is troublesome in a family, but in an organization, it can be disastrous. Lincoln knew the danger inherent in lies when he said, "No man has a good enough memory to make a successful liar."

On a plaque in Rockefeller Center are the following words which represent John D. Rockefeller's personal Credo: "I believe in the sacredness of a promise, that a man's word should be as good as his bond, that character, not wealth or power or position, is of supreme worth."

SECTION 15

THE ART OF
GETTING THINGS DONE

*"He that leaveth nothing to chance will do few things ill,
but he will do very few things."*
GEORGE SAVILE, MARQUESS DE HALIFAX, 1633–1695

"The man who can't dance thinks the band is no good."
POLISH PROVERB

"In a calm sea, every man is a pilot."
JOHN RAY, 1627–1705

*"Knowledge may give weight, but accomplishments give luster,
and many more people see than weigh."*
LORD PHILIP DORMER STANHOPE CHESTERFIELD, 1694–1773

*"He who is outside the door
already has the hard part of his journey behind him."*
DUTCH PROVERB

"Well Done is better than well said."
BENJAMIN FRANKLIN

THERE ARE THOSE WHO SPEND THEIR LIVES TRYING TO LOOK "COM-
POSED" IN SPITE OF THE FACT THAT NOTHING IS GETTING DONE. I call it
"profiling." Others flail about with their "hair on fire" making everything appear to be a crisis. Somewhere in between

there exists the "rational achiever" who continually gets the job done, knows when to react, recognizes a true crisis, and responds accordingly.

There is another type who is the consummate "prioritizer." He prioritizes every task. Whenever he is asked the status of a project, he uses his priorities as his excuse for not having the project completed. I am convinced that one can prioritize oneself into mediocrity.

The winner keeps all the "balls in the air" and will invariably show progress across the spectrum of his responsibilities. He is an expert at knocking out the easy ones while showing progress on the harder, long-term projects. The person who lists and performs all tasks in order of importance is the guy who takes two weeks to complete a 25-minute task because he prioritized it behind those tasks requiring 60 hours to complete. This individual has no idea how to manage his work and is destined for something less than mediocrity.

But there is the master of getting things done. He has an eye for problems. He senses when others are procrastinating or are unsure of the next step. This is the leader who "fixes things that are broken, corrects things that are bad, and changes things that are wrong" – without ever being told. By the grace of God, every organization should have at least one.

SECTION 16

JUST DO SOMETHING

*"...young leaders become servants of what is
rather than shapers of what might be."*
JOHN W. GARDNER

*"Real leaders create a sense of urgency.
If there is no crisis, they may create one."*
JIM BENSON

NOWHERE IS FAILURE TO TAKE THE INITIATIVE MORE IMPORTANT THAN
ON THE BATTLEFIELD. Most of us are aware of the frustra-
tions President Lincoln experienced in his efforts to find a
General Officer who would seize the initiative. Probably his
greatest frustration came with General George McClellan.
Loved by his men, superbly trained, and seemingly offen-
sive in style, he became the "splendid hesitator." And then
there was General Meade who failed to pursue General
Lee after success at Gettysburg, allowing Lee to cross the
Potomac River and extending the war. Finally, there was
Grant, admittedly not a tactician, but one who knew the
value of the initiative.

In the U.S. Marine Corps, we seldom bothered with
teaching the defense. Oh, we taught the troops how to

dig a foxhole, set up a perimeter defense, and how to plan and fire a final protective fire. The other 95 percent of our time was spent practicing how to attack from the sea, from the air, in the mountains, in the desert, and in the cities. I believe that is what has made the Corps what it is today; the nurtured mindset that it is an offensive force, which disdains anything less than complete victory.

In the work place, as on the battlefield, the winner is one who seizes the initiative, who is on the attack, and who possesses a bias for action as described by Peters and Waterman. We see this so-called initiative in many forms. We see it in the military officer or company manager who seizes upon a collateral duty that no one before him even touched. We see it in the new secretary who, without being told, completely reorganizes and dramatically improves the company files.

According to Elbert Hubbard, "The world bestows its big prizes in money and honors for but one thing, and that is initiative. And what is initiative? I'll tell you: it is doing the right thing without being told." On initiative, Mark McCormick says, "The projects people take on which are not part of their job description, which have not been assigned to them, are those projects for which people get the most recognition."

We have seen leaders who have a propensity for studying proposals to death. They suck the lifeblood out of winners. However, there are a significant number of large, complex, and successful organizations with an action bias that make things happen. Someone has termed this action orientation as Ready-Fire-Aim, which simply means "do something." Winners today initiate task forces, project centers, quality circles, and other short-term action teams to achieve progress and orchestrate change. These ad hoc organizations are seldom found in the organizational chart, and the membership is usually composed of those "who don't have the time." However, in organizations such as these with the right leadership, members are not constrained by job descriptions, organizational charts, or authority conflicts. They are given a task, a standard, and a timeline to "get it done."

The winner overcomes the status quo through action and seizure of the initiative. He surfaces in the organization because of his action bias and will try to overcome the naysayers who seek acclaim by raising questions and instilling doubt in others.

Real leaders create a sense of urgency within the organization. If there is no crisis, they may create one because they know that crises create stress and anxiety that produce adrenalin; adrenalin produces energy; and energy produces results.

SECTION 17

FAILURE IS ACCEPTABLE

*"Many of life's failures are people who did not realize
how close they were to success when they gave up."*
THOMAS A. EDISON

"Success is 99 percent failure."
SOICHIRO HONDA

*"If you want to launch big ships,
you have to go where the water is deep."*
CONRAD HILTON

MUCH HAS BEEN WRITTEN ABOUT HOW CONTEMPORARY COMPANIES
VALUE FAILURE AND THE ACCEPTANCE OF RISK. In fact, one could conclude that failure is valued if in the name of initiative. In my
research of the literature, I found nothing negative about
failure! I am a believer in change and fully realize that the
bold approach can lead to failure on occasion and, therefore, some failure has to be tolerated if an organization is to
be forward leaning. However, we must not lose sight of the
fact that repetitive failure will get you fired if it results from
inadequate research, failure to scan the environment, and to
effectively "what if" the possible outcomes of a proposal.

It would not be accurate to say that top executives hail failure, but they certainly recognize the benefits from it. Invariably, they perceive a failure as an opportunity and consistently use it as a "springboard" to reach higher goals. Since all learning involves some failure, Bennis and Nanus have surmised that reasonable failure is a prerequisite to success and should be perceived as so by modern managers.

One of Johnson & Johnson's directors, Jim Burke is quoted: "Any successful growth company is riddled with failure and there's just not any other way to do it....We love to win, but we also have to lose in order to grow."

Since failure is inevitable and in many cases a prerequisite to success, the leader must prepare the organization for defeat. This is particularly true in athletics, and I appreciate Bill Walsh's analogy.

> "When a wildebeest or zebra is finally entrapped by the lion, it submits to the inevitable – its head drops, its eyes glaze over, and it stands motionless and accepts its fate. The posture of defeat is also demonstrated by man – chin down, head dropped, shoulders visible as players leave the field in the later stages of the game when things are going against them. I often brought this to our players' attention using that example from nature, and we became very sensitive to it. I would assert, 'Even in the most impossible situations, stand tall, keep our heads up, shoulders back, keep moving, running, looking up, demonstrating our pride, dignity and defiance'."

So failure is often an unwelcome accomplice to success but can be the very springboard that permits success at a level never anticipated. Real leaders take failure in stride, stand tall and proud, as they advance in the pursuit of success in a new direction.

SECTION 18

IN ORDER TO WIN, LEARN HOW TO LOSE

"Fearful are the convulsions of defeat."
WINSTON CHURCHILL

LOSING AND FAILURE CAN BE THE SPRINGBOARD TO GREATER SUCCESS IF THE LEADER PREPARES THE ORGANIZATION FOR THE EVENTUALITY. The problem is exacerbated if the leader ridicules the unit or individuals after failure or loss. Of course, admonishment is in order and can be positive reinforcement if the failure results from lack of preparation, focus, or effort. Even then, the leader must accept some fault for the loss. The failure to prepare to lose is most evident in intercollegiate and professional athletics. Bill Walsh explained that, "Often in the NFL, you'll see teams start fast but then come apart when they lose a couple of games. That can result from a lack of ownership support, or from a coach ridiculing his players."

In the workplace, athletic field, or battlefield, the winner begins early on preparing the organization for the first setback. Otherwise, the organizational membership may resort to a mental letdown after defeat leading to sniping, finger-pointing, and grumbling that will surely affect the future in ways never anticipated.

SECTION 19

CONFORMITY AND RISK AVERSION

*"Our doubts are traitors, and make us lose
the good we oft might win, by fearing to attempt."*
WILLIAM SHAKESPEARE, 1564–1616

WINNERS RECOGNIZE THE DANGERS OF CONFORMITY. It is as much a symptom of fear of change as is jaw pain to an abscessed tooth. Conformity is the safe course of action. It is indicative of a personal lack of professional courage.

Not only do winners seek change makers, but they seek employees who possess the flexibility to recommit quickly when someone else initiates change.

Most success practitioners advocate change but little is said about the necessity for speed in initiating change. Rapid changes require rapid decision-making – yes, decision-making that is not laden with study after study and staff paper after staff paper. Rapid change results from streamlined staffing, clear and concise point papers, and staff presentations to the decision-makers that are to the point, convincing, and without bias. Perfection is the enemy of rapid change. Winners do not suffer those who resist and encumber changes for the sake of the status quo or the lack of professional courage.

I reserve the right to discriminate – to discriminate against those who are satisfied with the status quo, who are bound to the ways of the past, and who resist change solely because it involves risk and means work. They become enamored with the "way we have always done it" and resist the changes required to create growth and value. Bill Pollard, the insightful CEO of the highly successful Service Master Company wrote that, "The leader who makes things happen through others must learn to dip, upset, and redirect these activities of difference...." Conformity is the antithesis of change that leads to growth and success.

Risk, by its very nature, leads one to prefer conformity and the status quo. To overcome the fear associated with risk, the leader must immerse himself in reading, examination of the data, and new information, or else he will become "arrogant in his own ignorance," according to Pollard.

SECTION 20

CREATIVE LEADERS
ARE CHANGE-MAKERS

"Status quo is the enemy of change and hence, progress."
JIM BENSON

"The reasonable man adapts himself to the world;
the unreasonable man persists
in trying to adapt the world to himself.
Therefore, all progress depends on the unreasonable man."
GEORGE BERNARD SHAW

ADMIRAL HYMAN G. RICKOVER STATED, "THE DEEPEST JOY IN LIFE IS TO BE CREATIVE. To find an undeveloped situation, to see the possibilities, to decide upon a course of action, and then devote the whole of one's resources to carrying it out, even if it means battling against the stream of contemporary opinion, is a satisfaction in comparison with which superficial pleasures are trivial. But to create, you must care. You must be willing to speak out."

When change is required or one's vision dictates a better way of doing business, winners aren't afraid to swim against the tide. Additionally, they are people who are receptive to ideas for change coming up the chain of command. The winner is fearless in his quest for improvement.

We are all aware of the leader who, when confronted with a seemingly valid request for change, immediately begins to look for reasons why it won't work. On the contrary, winners look for the positives first. They immediately look for the benefits of a new way of doing business rather than looking for all the reasons why the new way won't work. Machiavelli, in *The Prince*, stated, "There is nothing more difficult to take in hand, more perilous to conduct, or more uncertain in its success, than to take the lead in the introduction of a new order of things."

According to Steven Brown, "The need for creativity runs through every segment of business. Management is essentially a 'thinking' job, not a 'doing' job. The lifeblood of any organization lies in ideas and creative thinking." Yet, invariably, the creative individual invites jealousy and resentment as well as sniping and criticism. Therefore, to create or advocate change, one has to be courageous. The winner prepares the battlefield for this resistance by building consensus before he springs his plan. Timing is critical. He knows that his chances for success are much higher if he is able to acquire support from some of the "movers and shakers" within the organization prior to proposing his plan for decision.

Resistance to change is not a new phenomenon. Attila the Hun, the barbaric but innovative Chieftain who reigned around 430 A.D., had a methodology for dealing with resistance. "We cannot expect to change our long-held traditions, to reorganize our army and to create great cities without internal opposition. Among you chieftains and Huns will be those whose spirits cling to our past ways.

We will show patience with you unenlightened ones. Yet, if you choose not our new cause and cause dissension, you will be stricken from our ranks."

Change is inevitable. Often it is the maverick who has the courage to advocate dramatic change. Yet, the maverick is often shunned and unpopular. He is often viewed as a "loose cannon" or an irrational and unreasonable person. According to George Bernard Shaw, "The reasonable man adapts himself to the world; the unreasonable man persists in trying to adapt the world to himself. Therefore, all progress depends on the unreasonable man." The winner cherishes the ideas of the maverick. He is listened to and encouraged to express his ideas. Change is a natural order within the unit; not change for the sake of change, but change for the sake of progress. Status quo is the enemy of change and hence, progress. The winner is an agent of change and will endure criticism and resistance in order to forge ahead and ensure victory.

SECTION 21

TIME MANAGEMENT

*"Do not sleep, lest you come to poverty; open your eyes,
and you will be satisfied with bread."*
PROVERBS 20:13

*"Time is the substance from which I am made.
Time is a river which carries me along, but I am the river;
it is a tiger that devours me, but I am the tiger;
it is the fire that consumes me, but I am the fire."*
JORGE LUIS BORGES

*"Heck by the time a man scratches his behind,
clears his throat, and tells me how smart he is,
we've already wasted fifteen minutes."*
LYNDON B. JOHNSON

*"In truth, people can generally make time for what they choose to do;
it is not really the time but the will that is lacking."*
SIR JOHN LUBBOCK

OVER THE YEARS, I HAVE REALIZED THE VALUE OF TIME AS A RESOURCE. Time is discussed to some degree in the next section on procrastination, but I believe a few thoughts on time as a resource are in order. Ben Franklin told us, "If time be of all things the most precious, wasting time must be, the greatest prodigality," Franklin also writes that, "lost time is never found again; and what we call time enough always proves too little."

Molloy wrote that, "Losers rarely take work home or work in places and at times not specifically designed for work. They rarely use spare time as work time. If the plane they are catching is going to be late, working in the airport will never occur to them." The winner realizes that if all administration is saved for the office setting, little time will be left to get out and about to view, hear, and sense the heartbeat of the unit. Hence, he seizes every opportunity to accomplish the administration of his position. He takes work home; he works in airports; and when he can find someone else to drive, he prepares while traveling from one meeting to the next.

Winners are masters at managing their time. They know that their discretionary time is limited and most of it will be spent keeping the organization running efficiently. Additionally, they avoid practices that waste the time of their subordinates such as overstaffing (which, seems to promote interacting rather than working), and holding an excessive number of meetings that are a concession to deficient organization.

Zig Zigler cautions that, "...time is generally wasted, lost, stolen, misplaced, or forgotten in minutes not hours." Have you ever noticed how few idle people there are in the first class section of an airplane? These are winners who know the value of the minute, have used it efficiently, turned it into success, and yes, often it means a seat in the first class section of the airplane.

JIM BENSON, MARY BENSON, GOLF-GREAT SAM SNEAD, LINDA BOWMAN AND VICE ADMIRAL SKIP BOWMAN AT RAY AND RUTH BUSSARD'S 50TH WEDDING ANNIVERSARY

SPECIAL FRIENDS — CHERRILL STONE, PHIL STONE AND JIM BENSON — 2000

COL JIM AND MARY BENSON IN CHICAGO–2002

LTCOL Jim Benson and Senator John Warner (VA) at Carlisle Barracks, PA–1987

2ND LT Jim Benson, Platoon Commander, 2nd Platoon, Company "I", 3rd Battalion, 1ST Marines in combat operations in Quang Nam Province, South Viet Nam, 1969

1ST LT JIM BENSON, COMPANY COMMANDER, COMPANY "I", 3RD BATTALION, 1ST MARINES AND KANHN, KIT CARSON SCOUT, QUANG NAM PROVINCE, SOUTH VIET NAM, 1970

LEFT TO RIGHT—JIM BENSON II (SON), CATHERINE BENSON (DAUGHTER), MARY BENSON (WIFE), AND COL JIM BENSON AT COL BENSON'S INSTALLATION AS PRESIDENT, MARION MILITARY INSTITUTE–2004

2nd LT JIM BENSON, PLATOON COMMANDER, 2nd PLATOON, COMPANY "I", 3rd BATTALION, 1st MARINES IN QUANG NAM PROVINCE, SOUTH VIET NAM–1969

SECTION 22

PROCRASTINATION

"Deadlines are the mother of invention."
JOHN M. SHANAHAN

"He who has begun is half done. Dare to be wise; begin!"
HORACE

*"Once men are caught up in an event, they cease to be afraid.
Only the unknown frightens men."*
ANTOINE DE SAINT-EXUPERY, 1900–1944

*"You don't hold your own in the world by standing on guard,
but by attacking and getting well hammered yourself."*
GEORGE BERNARD SHAW, 1856–1950

"All glory comes from daring to begin."
ANONYMOUS

*"There are 190 ways to beat,
but only one way to win; get there first."*
WILLIE SHOEMAKER

PEOPLE PROCRASTINATE ON DECISIONS BECAUSE THEY WANT MORE IN-
FORMATION; THEY PROCRASTINATE ON ACTIONS BECAUSE THEY FEAR
THE RISK. I call these people "thinking procrastinators." But
there exists another group of procrastinators who fail to

act because of apathy or lethargy. This group is hopeless in any discourse on success.

The winner possesses an instinct that tells him when enough information is available to make a decision and an inner confidence that permits him to act in spite of fear. He knows that tomorrow is not as good as today and when nothing is gained today, something is lost tomorrow.

Procrastination is a crippling disorder and a key ingredient of defeat. Its repercussions include stress and anxiety, which exponentially decrease one's chance for success even further. There are dozens of reasons to "wait" but few are legitimate. Some people procrastinate due to fear and doubt, lack of focus, distraction, lethargy, etc. Zig Zigler wrote that, "Someday Isle (someday I'll) is a nonexistent island. Someday Isle is one of the greatest excuses ever given. Tomorrow is the greatest labor-saving device ever brought to light."

What is it about youth that inherently includes a healthy dose of procrastination? The attitude that, "eventually I will feel like accomplishing this task or doing my homework" is a loony tune that has to be exorcised. No one "eventually" feels good about starting a dreaded task. In actuality, one finally starts the task when the pressure and anxiety rise to the point where one is urged into action. But it doesn't have to be that way. Zig Zigler put it as well as I've heard: "Don't wait until you feel like taking a positive action. Take the action and then you will feel like doing it." It is true, once we start the action, the progress itself motivates us to see it through.

My experience has been that a "do it now" leader is invariably successful. No matter the scenario, if one "what ifs" the downside or pejorative consequences, they are almost always minimized by early implementation. Furthermore, quick implementation beats the competition to the punch. Catching up with the competition is a real challenge. If we implement first, the competition has to react to our implementation (no matter how imperfect), while now we are already focusing on product improvement. It's like going on the offensive and seizing the initiative. We never give our competition time to figure out how to beat us because his time is consumed in catching up.

Some have called the "do it now" mentality the "hurry sickness." They claim that it is a disease that produces stress, unhappiness, and shortened longevity. A compulsive drive to beat the deadline, keep all the balls in the air, stay in the fast lane for promotion, and carry the day can be counter-productive if completely unreasonable and not balanced with exercise, a stable diet, and rest. However, to the winner, tomorrow exists only in the "long range" plan. All else is action, and action requires a "do it now" mentality. Winners recognize that tomorrow is the organization's single greatest impediment to success.

SECTION 23

NEVER TAKE COUNSEL
OF YOUR FEARS

"Boldness becomes rare, the higher the rank."
CARL VON CLAUSEWITZ

*"Winners create their own destiny by their proactivity
while losers suffer a fate by their reactivity."*
JIM BENSON

WINNING IS PERPETUAL AND SO ARE WINNERS! Those who expect to win, win, and continue to win. Those who spend their time trying not to lose are making the bed for their next defeat. Stonewall Jackson admonished his staff to "Never take counsel of your fears." Surely, General Jackson did not advocate reckless thinking without thought to the consequences. The great General was simply a believer in the initiative and understood the dangers of self-doubting and reservation.

Bennis and Nanus wrote of the "Wallenda Factor" and how shortly before Karl Wallenda fell to his death in 1978, he had been obsessed with the thought of falling and had taken extra precautions before that fateful 75-foot high-wire walk in San Juan, Puerto Rico. One might conclude that Wallenda had predestined his fall with his pre-occupation with not falling. On this one occasion, he took counsel of his fears to a degree never before observed in him by others. To the contrary, General Marshal Foch wrote to General Joffre in 1914, "My center gives way. My right recedes. The situation is excellent. I shall attack."

In conclusion, winners create their own destiny by their proactivity while losers suffer a fate by their reactivity.

SECTION 24

DRIVE

"Being defeated is often a temporary condition.
Giving up is what makes it permanent."
MARLENE VOS SAVANT

"If you start to take Vienna–take Vienna."
NAPOLÉON BONAPARTE

"There is no such thing as a great talent without great will-power."
HONORÉ DE BALZAR 1799–1850

"Give me all the 'wanna be's' you can find.
I'll take them all, for they are the 'gonna be's' of tomorrow."
JIM BENSON

CALL IT DRIVE, STEADFAST DETERMINATION, FIXITY OF PURPOSE, GRIT OR HEART, IT MAKES LITTLE DIFFERENCE; BUT IT IS THE PERSONAL CHARACTERISTIC THAT HAS MORE TO DO WITH WINNING THAN ANY I KNOW. Talent, intelligence, tact, knowledge, personal appearance, contacts, and opportunity are all important and contribute; but none are as important as the insatiable drive to succeed. General George S. Patton said it best, "How can anyone fail if he puts everything subordinate to success?"

We have all seen it in the classroom, on the athletic field, in the military, and in the business community, folks with ordinary ability but extraordinary desire succeed far above the expectations of others with exceptional ability and opportunity. During the past 20 years, we have observed and read many success stories wherein Vietnamese immigrants have come to this country with little or nothing other than the extraordinary desire to take advantage of the opportunities herein. With language barriers, little capital in most cases, few contacts, and no transportation, they have worked and saved until they could open their own businesses. Subsequently, they have poured their hearts and minds into their endeavors, reinvested the profits, and are already extremely successful even by U.S. standards. Likewise, their children graduate from our finest universities with an academic standing enviable by all. What is their secret? It's simple; their secret is the persistent determination to succeed.

The number one characteristic many leaders seek in a prospective employee is evidence of drive, persistence, and initiative. Evidence of these characteristics is seldom discernable in a resume. That is why references are so important. If drive or persistence is going to show up, the reference is where it will be. The wise executive requires references (or previous performance evaluations, if available) before he hires an employee for a key position.

The winner knows that when he finds an employee or player with drive, he also finds one with an exemplary work ethic, punctuality, and insistence on quality in all that he does. These characteristics manifest themselves in the eyes of others and tend to elevate the standards of performance of the entire unit or team.

It has become vogue to criticize the "wanna-be's" in today's society. Not me. I'm quick to respond, "give me all the 'wanna-be's' you can find. I'll take them all, for they are the 'gonna-be's' of tomorrow."

Not only do winners possess superior drive, but they are always on the lookout for others with the incessant determination to succeed. U.S. Marine Corps General Butch Neal of Gulf War fame once told me, "I recognize winners because they have a fire in their gut."

Winners are attuned to the words of Calvin Coolidge when he said,

Nothing in the world can take the place of persistence. Talent will not; nothing is more common than unsuccessful men of talent. Genius will not…the world is full of educated derelicts. Persistence and determination alone are omnipotent. The slogan 'press on' has solved and always will solve the problems of the human race.

There's no thrill in easy sailing when the skies are clear and blue, there's no joy in merely doing things which anyone can do. But there is some satisfaction that is mighty sweet to take, when you reach a destination that you thought you'd never make.
Spirella

SECTION 25

PRESS ON REGARDLESS

*"When everyone is against you,
it means that you are absolutely wrong–or absolutely right."*
ALBERT GUINON, 1863–1923

*"It's a little like wrestling a gorilla.
You don't quit when you're tired, you quit when the gorilla is tired."*
ROBERT STRAUSS

PROBABLY THE MOST PERSISTENT INDIVIDUAL I EVER MET WAS THE
FORMER SKIPPER OF THE U.S.S. OKLAHOMA CITY BACK IN THE MID-
1970s. Captain Paul D. Butcher, U.S. Navy, was a former
West Virginia school teacher and seaman recruit who
rose to the rank of Vice Admiral in the U.S. Navy. As the
Captain of the flagship of the United States 7th Fleet,
Captain Butcher was a taskmaster. His favorite phrase
was "press on regardless" and that is just what he did. He
failed selection to flag rank three times before making Rear
Admiral (one star) but then pressed on to Vice Admiral
(three stars) where he commanded the Military Sealift
Command and played a major role in transporting and re-
supplying U.S. forces in Saudi Arabia during Operations
Desert Shield and Desert Storm. In my judgment, Vice

Admiral Butcher was the epitome of persistence. Were this great American alive today, he would undoubtedly second Paul's challenge to the Philippians when he said, "But one thing I do: Forgetting what is behind and straining toward what is ahead, I press on toward the goal to win the prize" (Philippians 3:13-14).

It has been said that "those who fail in life often pursue the path of least persistence." It is troubling that many of our young choose the easiest school, the easiest major, and the easiest professors. Never mind what their talents are or what profession they are equipped for; their goal is just to get that sheepskin! They under sell themselves rather than pressing on toward a realistic goal. We see it in the workplace as well. Many workers strive for a position of less responsibility, easier hours, or less pressure.

Fear of failure, resistance to hard work, and the ever-present pursuit of free time are all contributors to this mentality. Where are the entrepreneurs who went bankrupt two and even three times before they made their mark? In life, when nothing is gained, something is lost. Leaders and managers must encourage the aggressive pursuit of progress. We must reward initiative, persistence, and uncommon achievement.

In my youth, I was dismayed over the luck of the prosperous. It seemed that the same coaches year in and year out got the break that permitted another championship. The same well-to-do businessman owned the seemingly worthless property that the new shopping center would be built on. It was years before it became abundantly clear that luck is the residue of diligence, and those who claim they never get a break wouldn't know an opportunity if it jumped out and mugged them.

General U. S. Grant preached that "In every battle there comes a time when both sides consider themselves beaten, then he who continues the attack wins." At Chancellorsville, General Lee claimed to be "too weak to defend, so I attacked." This is the type of persistence we need to beat the opposition in today's markets, gridirons, and battlefields.

Kipling captured the essence of persistence in two verses of his famous poem entitled "IF."

If you can make one heap of all your winnings
And risk it on one turn of pitch-and-toss,
And lose, and start again at your beginnings
And never breathe a word about your loss;
If you can force your heart and nerve and sinew
To serve your turn long after they are gone,
And so hold on when there is nothing in you
Except the Will which says to them: "Hold on!"
If you can talk with crowds and keep your virtue,

Or walk with Kings – not lose the common touch,
If neither foes nor loving friends can hurt you,
If all men count with you, but none too much;
If you can fill the unforgiving minute
With sixty seconds' worth of distance run,
Yours is the Earth and everything that's in it,
And – which is more – you'll be a Man, my son!

SECTION 26

PROVIDENCE

"I do not know beneath the sky nor on what seas shall be thy fate;
I only know it shall be high, I only know it shall be great."
RICHARD HOVEY

FOR THE TRUE WINNER, THERE IS DIVINE PROVIDENCE AND POWER, WHICH SUSTAINS HUMAN DESTINY. I can't explain it, but I know it's there. I have seen it time and time again. Is this divine guidance or answered prayer?

I am reminded of Conrad Hilton's experiences as he struggled in the early years in building his unprecedented hotel empire. "And each time the walls were about to close in and crush me, when there was no light for even one step ahead, 'something' happened – a bellboy thrust his life savings into my hand, a difficult business rival took everything I had with one hand and gave it back with the other, a promise that meant my business life was broken by one man and seven others stepped in to fill the breach. Could I take credit for personal cleverness in things like that? I could not. To me, they were answered prayer."

Colonel Joshua Chamberlain, the great Commander of the 20th Maine during the Civil War, President of Bowdoin College, and later Governor of Maine may have said it best,

"But what it is, I can't tell you. I haven't a particle of fanaticism in me. But I plead guilty to a sort of fatalism. I believe in a destiny – one, I mean, divinely appointed, and to which we are carried forward by a perfect trust in God. I do this, and I believe in it. I have laid plans, in my day, and good ones I thought. But they never succeeded. Something else, better, did, and I could see it plain as day, that God had done it, for my good."

SECTION 27

THE LEADER'S STANDARDS

"Ninety-nine and one-half just won't do–got to have a hundred."
WILSON PICKETT

JULES CAMBON SAID, "WE HAVE TO DEFEND THE COUNTRY AGAINST MEDIOCRITY: MEDIOCRITY OF SOUL, MEDIOCRITY OF IDEAS, MEDIOCRITY OF ACTION. We must also fight against it in ourselves."

Winners understand that most workers will rise to the standards to which they are held. If the standards are low, they will reach or slightly exceed them. If standards are high but reasonable, they will strive to attain them. Whether publicly stated or not, the membership of the unit or organization will quickly determine the leader's standards and expectations. Winners set the standards high and move the goalposts back, realizing that production of a quality product challenges the athletes, soldiers, or workers, enhances the reputation of the organization, and nurtures a winner's attitude throughout the work force.

Closely akin to expectations, the leader's standards are the critical ingredient to quality, excellence, and achievement in whatever the unit seeks to accomplish. However, standards must be enforced to have any affect on performance. Frequent restatement is also important to reseed the memory of the unit or company workers.

I love the Wilson Pickett song, "Ninety-nine and one-half just won't do – got to have a hundred." It says a lot about standards. People want to be a part of a winner. They want to be challenged. Nothing demotivates more than the failure of leadership to provide a challenge. Most of us perform better at full stretch. The feelings of accomplishment are self-perpetuating and lead to even greater levels of performance.

The winner is aware of the dangers inherent in setting standards that are not adhered to by management. According to Steven Brown, author of *Thirteen Errors Managers Make*, "Standards have the desired effect only if management practices what it preaches. We cannot say one thing and do another…announced standards not adhered to become pride destroyers rather than builders."

SECTION 28

SUPERVISION AND OVERSIGHT –
A PRELUDE TO SUCCESS

"An organization does well only those things the boss checks."
GENERAL BRUCE CLARK

"The eye of the master will do more work than both of his hands."
BENJAMIN FRANKLIN

ONE THING THE WINNER IS SURE OF IS THAT HE DOESN'T GET PAID FOR SIMPLY GIVING ORDERS. Probably one of the most significant weaknesses in American management is the misconception concerning giving orders. Many feel that they are paid to see what needs to be done and tell others to do it. I submit that less than 50 percent of the leader's salary is for recognizing what needs to be done and directing someone to do it. The remainder is for **ensuring** that the job is done and done to standard. I once heard Lieutenant General Sam Wilson, U. S. Army say, "In God I trust, everything else I check." Yes, the winner is a supervisor supreme. He is always observing, overseeing, and, where necessary, correcting. He knows that to walk by a problem is tantamount to endorsing it. Even where trust is high, supervision must exist; but it is a loose, coaching style of supervision.

The main job of managers is to ensure that the vision and intent of the executive leadership is being carried out. How many times have we seen the well-conceived Long-Range Plan gather dust as soon as it comes off the press? The winner ensures that the Long-Range Plan is implemented and that someone is assigned to see to it and to supervise implementation.

The military learned decades ago that futility is the lot of most orders without supervision. Additionally, organized feedback is frequently not dependable because no one wants to give the boss bad news. Hence, the only truly reliable feedback is to go out and look yourself. It is not a matter of distrusting subordinates; it's a matter of distrusting communications. Failure to see for oneself is the primary reason for persisting on a course of action long after it has ceased to be effective. According to Peter Drucker, "One needs organized information for the feedback. One needs reports and figures. But unless one builds one's feedback around direct exposure to reality – unless one disciplines oneself to go out and look – one condemns oneself to a sterile dogmatism and with it, to ineffectiveness."

Peters and Austin defined Management By Walking Around (MBWA) as a common sense leadership formula, which ensures management's knowledge of workers, customers, and problems. MBWA keeps the winner in touch. It allows him a chance to listen and empathize with the workforce. Winners get out of their offices and expect subordinate managers to do the same. Seeing is better than any computer printout, and it is not hearsay. MBWA leads to innovation and rapid problem solving because the existence of the problem is discovered sooner.

MBWA is as valuable in the textile plant and modern university as in a military organization. The winner gets out of the office and gets the pulse of the organization. It has been my experience as a battalion executive officer and a regimental commander that seldom was there an instance when I visited the various commodity sections (motor transport, communications, supply or medical) or the barracks and talked to the troops and non-commissioned officers that I didn't learn something that I should act upon. And as Poor Richard tells us, "The eye of the master will do more work than both of his hands."

SECTION 29

DISCIPLINE AT HOME AND AT WORK

"Nothing emboldens sin so much as mercy."
WILLIAM SHAKESPEARE, 1564–1616

"Part of being good is looking good."
JIM BENSON

*"Self-discipline is that which, next to virtue,
truly and essentially raises one man above the other."*
JOSEPH ADDISON

THERE EXISTS ORGANIZATIONAL DISCIPLINE AND INDIVIDUAL SELF-DISCIPLINE. Both are established by resolute leadership either in the family, the unit, or workplace.

According to John Rosemond, psychologist, writing for the Richmond Times-Dispatch, discipline is compelling – not persuasive. Discipline is unequivocal; it's not about rules and legalism. It is about leadership, teaching, command, and communications. It involves compassion, firmness, and the appropriate use of consequences. In the unit or workplace, it involves order, synergy, and exactness. After my many years as a Marine officer, I can spend

30 minutes in a military unit, school, or company and tell something about the leader, his standards, and the discipline within the organization. Order and appearance are constants in winning organizations.

Disciplined organizations are distinguished by accountability. People are held accountable for their work. The leader leaves no doubt who is responsible for what task and is resolute in expecting the task to be accomplished to standard and on time. If it is not completed to his liking, the responsible individual receives a private word of reproof minimally.

Undoubtedly, one of the most difficult challenges facing the leader is where to draw the line on discipline. Military discipline is exacting and enforced by more severe consequences. In the civilian workplace, one finds a more relaxed environment where some freedom exists particularly in personal appearance and dress. I have always been disappointed in the example set by professional athletes and the tolerance exhibited by the ownership of professional teams. Dennis Rodman of the Chicago Bulls fame comes to mind. His tattooed body, colored hair, and unshaven appearance said something about the standards set by the ownership. In contrast, New York Yankees owner George Steinbrenner has a different set of standards as observed when future Hall of Fame pitcher Randy Johnson was directed to cut his locks when traded to the Yankees.

I am reminded of two professors at a private liberal arts college where I once served as a vice president. Both prided themselves in their individuality demonstrated by their long hair, wrinkled and faded blue jeans, sandals, and unshaven appearance. I recall the president's lament that he could never send them off campus to represent the institution. In fact, if he could have hidden them on campus during alumni weekend and open house, he would have done so. As they basked in their individuality, neither realized that they were two of the lowest paid faculty members on campus.

I have always been taken by the wisdom and thinking of the great sailor, John Paul Jones. His treatise on accountability, discipline, and the manner of a leader is timeless.

> It is by no means enough that an officer of the Navy should be a capable mariner. He must be that, of course, but also a great deal more. He should be, as well, a gentleman of liberal education, refined manner, punctilious courtesy, and the nicest sense of honor. He should not only be able to express himself clearly and with force in his own language both with tongue and pen, but he should be versed in French and Spanish.
>
> He should be the soul of tact, patience, justice, firmness and charity. No meritorious act of a subordinate should escape his attention or be let pass without its reward, if even the reward be only one word of approval. Conversely, he should not be blind to a single fault in any subordinate, though at the same time he should be quick and unfailing to distinguish error from malice, thoughtlessness from incompetency, and well-meant shortcoming from heedless or stupid blunder. As he should be universal and impartial in his rewards and approval of merit, so should he be judicial and unbending in his punishment or reproof of misconduct.
> *John Paul Jones*

SECTION 30

BALANCED EXCELLENCE

"In the race for quality (excellence), there is no finish line."
DAVID KEARNS, FORMER CEO OF XEROX

"BALANCED EXCELLENCE" IS A CONCEPT FOR WINNERS. I first heard of it from U. S. Marine Colonel Hank Stackpole (later to rise to the rank of Lieutenant General). According to then Colonel Stackpole, the winner strives to excel across the spectrum of his span of control. Likewise, a battalion commander I worked for in Viet Nam used to preach that "if we took care of the little things, the big things would take care of themselves." His theory seemed to bear fruit for as he berated us about things that were perceived as trivial to the officers of the battalion, the battalion performed superbly in the field, accumulating amazing statistics in weapons and prisoners of war captured, and enemy killed in action while maintaining a low friendly casualty rate.

A Balanced Excellence approach to one's duties, if applied conscientiously, will result in recognition in areas never conceived beforehand. The winner strives for first place in every endeavor. He, therefore, receives much recognition, is soon widely respected, and his pursuit of excellence across the spectrum of his duties leads him to positions of greater responsibility and, hence, greater recognition. It doesn't take a mathematics wizard to see the exponential gains in recognition and respect acquired by the winner as he pursues excellence across a broad spectrum of his activities.

SECTION 31

COMPLACENCY – PLATEAUING – PLUNGING

"Never mistake motion for action."
ERNEST HEMINGWAY

COMPLACENCY, SUBSEQUENT TO SUCCESS, RESULTS IN PLATEAUING. According to Robert Kriegel, *If It Ain't Broke...Break It,* "plateauing occurs when the individual or the organization stops growing and moving upward. In fact, experience shows that plunging quickly follows plateauing." We have all seen this in the workplace as well as on the athletic field. When winners begin to feel comfortable with their performance or the performance of their unit, the warning light comes on. Experience and instinct tell them that when all seems to be running well, when their comfort level begins to peg, it is time to get out of the office and exercise their curiosity. Invariably, something has gone awry, and, by talking to the rank and file, they invariably head off the problem before plateauing turns to plunging.

According to Robert Townsend, managers tend to make their biggest mistakes in things they've previously done best. In business, as elsewhere, hubris is the unforgivable sin of acting cocky when things are going well. As the Greeks tiresomely told us, "hubris is followed inexorably and inevitably by nemesis."

Personal experiences as a commander in the U. S. Marine Corps taught me that whenever I came to believe that my unit was at the summit in terms of performance, something serious was already occurring in the bowels of the organization that would soon upset my euphoria. In time, I became a bit of a pessimist, and whenever my ego began to peg, I quickly began to personally investigate by talking to folks two levels down in the unit. Usually, I could find some festering problem whether it was a racial misunderstanding, a leadership issue in a subordinate unit, or a morale problem that had not reached my level. Of course, discovering the problem early simplifies its resolution.

Some have written recently that pessimists tend to be effective leaders. In my judgment, there is truth in the theory. It might be better stated that experience enhances one's ability to lead effectively because it nurtures ever-present doubt and causes one to constantly "what if" the environment for potential problems.

SECTION 32

TITHE TO LEARNING

*"However, the most notable trait of great leaders,
certainly of great change leaders, is their quest for learning."*
"WINNING AT CHANGE," *LEADER TO LEADER*, **NUMBER 10, FALL 1998, P. 32**

"Originality is nothing but judicious imitation."
VOLTAIRE (FRANCOIS MARIE AROULET), 1694–1778.

"It's but little good you'll do watering the last year's crops."
GEORGE ELIOT (MARIAN EVANS CROSS), 1819–1880.

"If you think education is expensive–try ignorance."
DEREK BOK

SOME YEARS AGO WHILE ATTENDING A COURSE ON CRISIS ACTION PLANNING, I HEARD RETIRED U.S. ARMY LIEUTENANT GENERAL SAM WILSON SPEAK. General Wilson later became the President of Hampden-Sidney College in Farmville, Virginia.

He is well known as one of the infamous Merrill's Marauders of World War II fame, a former Deputy Director of the Central Intelligence Agency, and once the Director of the Defense Intelligence Agency. He admonished us "to devote 10 percent of our time to learning, be it formal professional education, individual study, or just plain reading."

When Bennis and Nanus asked their research subjects about the personal qualities necessary for success, little was said regarding charisma, dress, intellect, or time management. More than any other qualities, they said that successful managers are perpetual learners. In today's changing environment, those who are not continually stretching, growing, and striving for knowledge do not survive.

Some would conclude that television has supplanted books as the primary attitude developer or attitude changer in America. This is probably the case in the lives of too many Americans who have completed their formal education. It is hard to argue the role that television plays in the perception of current events in this country. But one has to stretch the truth to categorize television as a prominent educational tool in the American home. As Marya Mannes wrote, "a person can be fascinated by movies and diverted by television, but they are a series of snacks. Books are the real nourishment of the human mind."

General Motors has learned the lesson of customer satisfaction the hard way. At Saturn, employees dedicate 5 percent of their workday to training. Although not a tithe per se, this is certainly a commitment to learning.

To be successful in today's world one must be current in the profession of choice. The only way to stay current is through study and reading. A continuous thesis of this book is the importance of the study of man. One need not read from only the writings of those in his or her profession. In fact, the contrary is true. Leaders and managers in the private and public sectors can learn from the writings of General George Patton, Admiral Hyman Rickover, as well as Peter Drucker, and the late Harold Geneen. Military leaders can learn from the likes of Mike McCormick, Norman Vincent Peale, and Harvey Mackay. All can learn from the master of human skills as portrayed so well by Donald T. Phillips in his *Lincoln on Leadership*.

The art of leading is not something that is accomplished in a weeklong seminar or weekly one-hour training sessions. Leadership training involves continuous instruction, practical on-the-job experience, and years of self-study of books and periodicals on the techniques and philosophies of proven leaders. It is well known that leaders are not born, but made. Although appearance, intelligence, and charisma make it easier for some to lead than others, we can all learn to lead if we are willing to pay the price in terms of education.

Those who are well read and educated in their choice of endeavor and the art of leadership seem to be more confident in their environment and innovative in their approach to their jobs. They appear to be less imprisoned by their paradigms than the less informed. Education seems to filter new information through the paradigm making change less fearsome. The world is full of "copy cat thinkers." Successful leaders and managers seize the initiative through confidence acquired through the pursuit of knowledge. "Tell me what you read," observed Goethe, "and I will tell you what you are."

SECTION 33

THE SCHOOL AND ITS CUSTOMER

"Service is just a day-in, day-out, ongoing, never-ending, unremitting, persevering, compassionate type of activity."
LEON GORMAN

IF THERE IS ANYTHING I HAVE TAKEN FROM W. EDWARDS DEMING'S TOTAL QUALITY MANAGEMENT (TQM), IT IS THAT MANY ORGANIZATIONS DO NOT KNOW THE IDENTITY OF THEIR CUSTOMER. As a former secondary public school teacher and presently the president of a military junior college and preparatory school, I quickly recognize schools that put their students first – schools that genuinely care about the attitudes and achievements of all of their students. As a general rule, private institutions walk the extra mile to ensure student learning and parental feedback. Private schools realize that the student and his parents are their customers. Generally, students are treated with care; parents receive frequent written and oral feedback; and the administration and faculty see to those things that ensure the student wants to return each year. Why? Because the students are their customers and economic engine, and they know it. I realize that customer is not a coveted term among teachers because of its business or economic connotation, and I do not care if one substitutes client for customer. But the truth is that the student is the one served by our schools. His development is the school's mission and the reason for its existence.

I have observed public schools where the attitude of the faculty was as if the student were fortunate to be there, and it was his responsibility to come in motivated to learn. Teachers provide the material and if the student does not care to receive it, so be it. This is not to criticize public schools, because I believe in public schools, and I realize that the public schools have many extraordinary teachers. I only draw on the comparison of public versus private because of the necessity for private schools to see the student and his parents as "the" customer.

I have observed some professors at fine colleges whose primary focus was on their "A" students. They would adopt the young intellectual and use him in research projects and speak of his abilities publicly. However, I am more interested in the average and below average student with drive and ambition or the lack thereof because of the absence of opportunity. Most professors can teach the bright and handsome child from the stable home who is motivated for college. His parents are probably college graduates and prominent in the community. But, I am drawn to the professors who thrive on the leadership challenge of motivating and teaching the unkempt, not-so-bright student who comes to college disinterested, distracted, moody, and even disruptive. Some of these students are athletes and are in college simply to play ball. They should be viewed by faculty members as an opportunity to turn on the light of education.

Somehow, we have to make school something that young people anticipate with enthusiasm. The atmosphere has to be that the student is special; that he is the object of our attention; and that the rules are there to make school a positive experience for him. Great effort must be exerted to ensure he knows that the entire faculty is there to help him and genuinely cares whether he succeeds. But this is not to say that the administration must be tolerant of inappropriate behavior. In fact, inappropriate behavior must be addressed by firm and consistent sanctions to include suspension from school. Sometimes when sanctions or punishments are levied, "administrators are not doing it to them – but for them."

This is but one example of an organization that often has not always determined its customer. The winner knows whom he has to please to be successful. The winning principal or college administrator who has bathed himself in student and parent feedback will reap the benefits scholastically, academically, and in the resultant achievement tests in which his students frequently distinguish themselves.

It is not surprising that so many leaders are great teachers because that is what leadership is all about–helping others–helping others perform closer to their God-given abilities.

SECTION 34

STRATEGIC AND LONG RANGE PLANNING

"No plan survives contact with the enemy."
FIELD MARSHAL HELMUTH CARL BERNARD VON MOLTKE

*"Intricate and complex are recipes for failure
in organizational planning."*
JIM BENSON

WINNING AND SUCCESS IN THE WORKPLACE, ATHLETIC FIELD, OR BATTLEFIELD ARE CLOSELY CORRELATED WITH EFFECTIVE EXECUTION OF THE PLAN OF ACTION. Likewise, the quality of execution is correlated with the simplicity of the plan. Intricate and complex are recipes for failure in organizational planning.

In combat, planning is central to everything that is done. Typically at division level and higher, the operations officer and his staff are planning the next two days of operations. Often, another group of planners is planning the battle three days out and more. At battalion, company, and platoon level, daily planning occurs, which coordinates all unit movements to include a fire support plan and a rudimentary logistics and communications plan. In the air, each flight is carefully planned and briefed. I am less familiar with Navy planning, but am sure that it is also based on the KISS (keep it simple, stupid) principle.

Strategic military plans and campaigns are implemented as conceived with as few changes as possible because of the coordination necessary and mutual support inherent in these types of plans. However, since it is rare that planning precisely predicts the actions of the enemy, strategic plans are generally trashed by the end of day two of the campaign and often serve only to get the friendly force ashore or on the ground prepared to fight. From then on its daily operational planning that carries the fight to the enemy.

Corporate strategic planning is another animal indeed. Similar to the military strategic plan, principal staff members, department heads, and other executives come together to create the vision, mission, guiding principles, and goals of the organization. Strategic planning often purports to be a tool for organizational change. Unfortunately, after arguing for 5–14 days, a plan replete with compromise is often agreed to only to be relegated to the shelf, never to be seen again. Nonetheless, the exercise of strategic planning has value as it creates a singleness of purpose and a knowledge of the mission and values of the organization not well understood before the advent of the planning process.

SECTION 35

DECISION-MAKING

*"Life is the art of drawing sufficient conclusions
from insufficient premises."*
SAMUEL BUTLER

*"An executive is a man who decides; sometimes he decides right,
but always he decides."*
JOHN H. PATTERSON

*"The man who insists upon seeing with perfect clearness
before he decides, never decides."*
HENRI FREDERIC AMIEL, 1821–1881

*"Soon after a hard decision, something inevitably occurs to cast doubt.
Holding steady against that doubt usually proves the decision."*
R. I. FITZHENRY, 1918–

*"Decide promptly, but never give any reasons. Your decisions
may be right, but your reasons are sure to be wrong."*
LORD WILLIAM MURRAY MANSFIELD, 1705–1793

*"Never explain. Your friends do not need it
and your enemies will not believe it anyway."*
ELBERT HUBBARD, 1856–1915

EFFECTIVE DECISION-MAKING IS THE SWORD OF THE WINNER. The winner is trained to assimilate large amounts of data, organize it mentally, quickly cost/benefit it, and make a rational decision.

111

Additionally, he can take small amounts of data, quickly rationalize it, cost-benefit it, and make a timely rational decision. In reality, most decisions are of the latter type. Hence, the winner is capable of making numerous critical and timely decisions under pressure in the heat of the moment, and those decisions are often the ones which carry the day.

Winners realize that, most of the time, not all of the desired data is available to facilitate a decision. However, they have learned to trust their instincts. They sense when sufficient data is available and when to step back and ask more questions. Robert Ringer's *The Natural Law of Balance* says, "the universe is in balance...you should never delude yourself about the reality that you must always give up something in order to gain something. If you can't see one or more offsets when making a decision, you'd best call time-out and study the situation more carefully, because it probably means that you're overlooking more important facts."

What can be more frustrating than to work for a leader or manager who lacks the confidence to make timely decisions? He is the same procrastinator who won't act until every element of data is received. He relishes in committees, boards, and study groups, as they are his way of delay and disguise his lack of courage and confidence. He invariably employs consensus decision-making, which may only maintain the status quo and can be a play-it-safe methodology, which, if over used, can guarantee mediocrity.

My intent is not to criticize the thorough, deliberate, and organized decision-maker who refuses to act when more and better information is available and the staff has failed to provide it. Furthermore, I realize that the world is also full of impulsive, hip-shooters who react with little or no information and are the antithesis of the winner. I simply want to shock the procrastinator into action and help him realize that winners must routinely make decisions when not all the data is in. The acceptance of risk is the natural order of the day for leaders. Failure to act in a timely manner is tantamount to defeat in business, the public sector, politics, war, and athletics.

The environment has much to do with the leader's willingness to accept risk. His perception of how he is viewed by the organizational hierarchy, the media, the public, his subordinates, and even his peers, all impact on his willingness to trust his instincts and be decisive. For example, when General Meade assumed command of the Army of the Potomac in June, 1863, General Lee knew that Meade would be cautious until he was more comfortable in his new position. On the other hand, General Lee was confident in his position; hence, he assumed great risk in attacking Meade's Army over open terrain and was, henceforth, dealt a resounding defeat at Gettysburg.

Winners recognize that a decision is only as good as the information on which it is based. They know how to get the facts by asking the right questions that drive straight to the heart of the matter. They sense when a subordinate is hedging or avoiding the hard question either because he does not know the answer or because the answer is unpleasant. It doesn't take the winner long to plot the reliability and dependability of the members of his staff. He knows who to query thoroughly and who to accept at face value. According to Euripides (485–406 BC), "a man's most valuable trait is a judicious sense of what not to believe."

The winner will not routinely make his decisions based on input from one level down. He gets to know people two levels down and often gets first-hand facts from the rank and file. He realizes that the lower he goes for information, the less tainted it becomes. The mere fact that he goes down two or more levels for his information does much to keep his staff on their toes. It does wonders for the morale and attitude of the junior leadership and rank and file to know that their opinions count, especially when their comments are clearly portrayed in the final decision.

Organizational hierarchy is in itself inimical to efficient decision-making. As decision or issue papers work their way up the chain of command, with review and recommendation attached at every level, time and money are lost. The winner realizes this and empowers his subordinate leaders and managers to make decisions at the lowest level possible.

The one type of decision, which always requires patience and forethought, is a decision concerning firing, transferring, or promoting personnel. Firing personnel is discussed in Section 5, so I will not address it here again. Through the years I have observed many leaders move people at will in organizations, and I have come to the conclusion that the turbulence and loss of continuity in such madness is extremely costly in terms of organizational efficiency. Winners contemplate personnel decisions carefully and act only when reasonably certain that the turbulence and loss of continuity associated with the move will pay dividends in the long run. They are cognizant of the costs inherent in moving personnel and reflect on all the competing courses of action before executing personnel decisions.

SECTION 36

DELEGATING

"Delegate but don't abdicate."
ANONYMOUS

"There is a difference between being in control and controlling."
JIM BENSON

DELEGATING IS THE PROCESS OF PREPARING OTHERS TO ASSUME MORE RE-SPONSIBILITY. Real leaders realize that success is possible only if the entire organization performs. Nevertheless, egos tend to get in the way, and many are never able to adequately delegate authority. Real leaders will find ego gratification in developing, directing, and observing subordinates assume responsibility and achieve success on their own.

The criteria for delegation seems to be more intuitive than intellectual. The following criteria seem to prevail:

- Trust and confidence in subordinates.

- Risk associated with authority delegated.

- The greater the organizational complexity – the greater the delegation.

- Available time – less delegation occurs during crisis management.

I have always had more confidence in the written word than the spoken word. It probably dates back to my time as a platoon and company commander in Viet Nam where misunderstanding of orders could be deadly. Since then, I have concluded that some people simply do not take verbal direction as official, or at least, as serious as written direction. Someone said that the nerves leading from the eye to the brain are many times more sensitive than those leading from the ear to the brain. So, if you expect compliance to your directions, reduce them to writing—clear, concise, and explicit.

With the above as a backdrop, delegation is a key ingredient to winning. It is becoming increasingly difficult for leaders and managers in most organizations to juggle all the balls simultaneously. If it were possible, it wouldn't be necessary to have assistants, deputies, and staffs.

SECTION 37

PICK YOUR BATTLES CAREFULLY

"Pick battles big enough to matter, small enough to win."
JONATHON KOZOL

WINNERS REALIZE THAT IT IS COUNTERPRODUCTIVE TO TAKE ON EVERY IS-
SUE VEHEMENTLY EVEN WHEN THEY ARE SURE THEIR POSITION IS THE COR-
RECT ONE. We have all seen those who are always looking for
a fight and will go to the mat on the slightest of issues. These
are the ones who are referred to as obstinate, hard-headed,
rigid, and too disruptive and contentious for positions of
greater responsibility. Winners have learned the value of
compromise even when they believe strongly in their position. They realize that consensus is not always possible.

Winners examine issues to determine their long-term rele-
vancy. They know that sometimes it is better to intentionally
give in on one or two lesser issues in order to put themselves
in a better bargaining position for the "real" issue(s).

The following guidelines are appropriate for winners:
- Pick your battles carefully; there will be times to go to
  the mat but they must be judiciously selected.

- Don't fight when you can't win.
- Compromise when the issue is gray.
- Show humility when you win.

The best that one can expect is to win **most of the time** when one is right! Winners realize this and know that those who pick their battles indiscriminately seldom attain a position where they get the opportunity to fight for or influence the real issues.

SECTION 38

PICK YOUR ENEMIES WITH CARE

"You saw his weakness, and he will never forgive you."
JOHANN CHRISTOPH FRIEDRICH VON SCHILLER, **1775–1854**

*"He who has a thousand friends has not a friend to spare,
and he who has one enemy will meet him everywhere."*
ALI IBN-ABI-TALIB, C. **602–661**

"A man cannot be too careful in the choice of his enemies."
OSCAR WILDER, **1854–1900**

*"Anyone can become angry–that is easy.
But to be angry with the right person, to the right degree,
at the right time, for the right purpose, and in the right way–
that is not easy."*
ARISTOTLE

WINNERS NEVER MAKE AN ENEMY UNLESS THEY DEEM IT NECESSARY. They realize that whenever one intentionally makes an enemy, he unintentionally makes several others. According to Harvey Mackey, "The clubhouse men of the world are just waiting for a chance to kick you in the ass. You may not be watching them, but they're watching you, and the more arrogant you are, whether you're an eleven-year-old kid or some self-important business type, the better the odds they'll find a way to get even." Of course, there are times when it is necessary to make an enemy, but indiscriminate statements and actions which alienate others are wrought with consequences. And if there are nicks in one's armor, rest assured that every enemy will find them and exploit them.

One of the deadliest enemy makers in an organization is gossip. Additionally, it is one of the primary perpetrators of division within a unit. It is an enemy producer of the highest order. As the old saying goes, "bad talk always comes back." Solomon was right on the mark in Proverbs 10:18, "…whoever spreads slander is a fool." Winners don't participate in gossip!

Winners use confrontation judiciously. Confrontation, especially public confrontation, causes friction within the organization. It often leads to the choosing of sides and can cause lasting resentment that is detrimental to the organization as a team. At times, confrontation is necessary, but the winner will employ it sparingly and privately when it becomes the only viable option. According to Attila the Hun, as translated by Wess Roberts in his priceless little book, *Leadership Secrets of Attila the Hun*, "Chieftains should never rush into confrontation."

While it is important not to make enemies external to the organization, it is also important to minimize enemies inside the organization—yes, even if you are the boss. Again, I draw on the writings of Harvey Mackey. He says the winner is never his own hatchet man. As the head of the organization, "you have to get someone who can make the tough, mean, unpopular decisions and can take the fall when they get too tough, mean, and unpopular." Likewise, he advises if you choose to be the hatchet man in spite of his advice to the contrary, you had better possess the following:

- "exceptional intelligence with the ability to ask tough questions from 9:00 AM until quitting time, whenever that is;
- fair-mindedness (you might call it the ability to hit with either a left jab or a right cross);
- maintenance of extremely high performance standards for yourself;
- commitment to keep your guard up continually (and cynically);
- ability to shed criticism like a duck shedding raindrops"

As one can see, few of us have our act wound so tight that we can afford to continually be our own hatchet man because of the emotional and political price we must pay.

And, to reinforce my point, I will quote one more winner. According to Bill Walsh, the former head coach of the three-time Super Bowl Champion San Francisco 49ers, "In building the organization, I also stressed the importance of not making enemies. We didn't want to expend energy on anything other than the project at hand. We couldn't afford an enemy, whether it was NFL coaches and management, league employees, players, the press, college coaches, and local citizens. One enemy could do more damage than the good done by a hundred friends."

SECTION 39

NEGOTIATIONS

*"The fellow who says he'll meet you halfway
usually thinks he is standing on the dividing line."*
ORLANDO A. BATTISTO

"Deliberation is the work of many men. Action, of one alone."
CHARLES DE GAULLE

WHILE SERVING AS THE CHIEF, PLANS AND FORCE DEVELOPMENT, J-5, U. S. SOUTHERN COMMAND, I LED THE PLANNING EFFORT FOR SEVEN MILITARY CONTINGENCY PLANS FOR CENTRAL AND SOUTH AMERICA. This planning occurred in the mid-1980s when communist insurgencies were replete throughout the region. Nicaragua planning was particularly contentious, and there were strong indicators that we might have to deploy a very significant force seizing the beaches, airfields, and evacuating U. S. citizens from many parts of the country.

Sometimes it could take a year to complete a controversial plan like the Nicaragua plan. The four military services would fight like cats over their role and the size of their force. There were many meetings, and they were all classified Top Secret. I would become extremely agitated with the dissent and obstinate positions of the services on the first day of each meeting. Clearly, each service planner came with an agenda. Of course, all considered themselves tacticians and had a better plan centered on their own force capabilities. However, the Commander-in-Chief of the Southern Command was a four-star General Officer, and I had his guidance before I ever went to each meeting. After the first day firefight between the services and the realization that we would not budge on the concept of operations, planners would return on day two, and we would make significant progress. I recall Colonel Bill Comee's counsel–"Jim, the first day is always the 'mating dance'."

Winners never set their expectations too high for the first day of any serious or protracted negotiation. They realize that the first day is generally "the mating dance" where the "Cahunas" spar; by the second day, things begin to break.

SECTION 40

COMMS CHECK

"Communications dominate war;
broadly considered,
they are the most important single element in strategy,
political or military."
Alfred T. Mahan

Benjamin Disraeli wrote that, "one writes not simply to be understood but not to be misunderstood." We have all written something that made perfect sense to us, and yet it was completely misconstrued by the reader to our dismay. I recall the colossal breakdown in corporate communications when General Motors attempted to market the Chevy Nova in Latin America, not realizing that "no va" meant "it won't go" in Spanish.

I suggest that no profession is so replete with the necessity to think and write coherently than the military. Military operations must be clearly understood by every subordinate element because clarity can determine victory or defeat and life or death. Some are still debating Jeb Stuart's misunderstanding of Robert E. Lee's orders at Calvary Field at Gettysburg, which may have cost Lee the battle and the South the war. Of course, NASA and other scientists must write effectively, and doctors must write clinically. However, I am convinced that the legal profession never heard of Disraeli. One should see the language in some of the lawyer produced contracts that I have to try to understand.

SECTION 41

PROBLEMS AND ISSUES

"A problem clearly stated is a problem half solved."
DOROTHEA BRANDE

*"Focus 90 percent of your time on solutions
and only 10% of your time on problems."*
ANTHONY J. D'ANGELO

WINNERS DO NOT SUFFER STAFF MEMBERS WHO CONTINUALLY PRES-
ENT PROBLEMS AND ISSUES WITHOUT SIMULTANEOUSLY BRINGING AL-
TERNATIVES AND A RECOMMENDED COURSE OF ACTION TO SOLVE THE
PROBLEM OR ISSUE. Someone once said that the problem is
half solved once it is defined. Problems are best solved at
the lowest level possible. Leaders who shoot from the hip
and personally tackle each problem with minimal input will
suffer much from their exuberance. The staff will gladly
pass the problem up and, hence, the responsibility for the
results. But winners resist the temptation to immediately
respond; they wait for the courses of action and pros and
cons of each. Try this technique; you will be surprised how
often your decision differs from your initial reaction when
you were originally presented with the problem or issue.

SECTION 42

RECIPROCITY IN HUMAN INTERACTION

"A generous man will prosper;
he who refreshes others will himself be refreshed."
PROVERBS 12:25

REAL WINNERS ARE UNSELFISH! They have an inherent character, which is giving in nature. Somehow, they have acquired an understanding that one reaps what one sows. Organizations revolve around personal relationships. These relationships are created in a myriad of ways. The magic about genuine, unselfish behavior demonstrated by winners is that it is reciprocated. Solomon confirmed the principle of reciprocity in Proverbs 12:25 when he said, "a generous man will prosper; he who refreshes others will himself be refreshed." Emerson reinforced the principle; "It is one of the most beautiful compensations of this life that no man can sincerely try to help another without helping himself."

In spite of the evidence confirming these principles of successful living, one of the toughest challenges in this life is to speak highly of and, yes, assist one's contemporaries and competitors. But "true" and "respected" winners will not denigrate or criticize contemporaries or competitors for personal gain.

According to Robert Townsend, "Every success I've ever had came about because I was trying to help other people. Every promotion I got at American Express came about when I was up to my ears helping my associates be as effective as possible.... On the other hand, every time I had a really clever idea for making me a lot of money or for getting me into some interesting job, it turned out to be an utter failure."

Winners develop a habit of helping others and not for personal gain. It can be a struggle, and one has to work at it continually until it becomes habitual. If you want to be a winner, try this:

- Do something for somebody in the organization daily.
- Never pass up an opportunity to help another or speak highly of another, and do so for contemporaries as well as competitors.

Try it for a week; you'll be amazed at the results!

SECTION 43

TRUST YOUR INSTINCTS

"Instinct is untaught ability."
ALEXANDER BAIN

"Instinct is the nose of the mind."
MADAME DE GIRARDIN

*"If necessity is the mother of invention,
intuition is the mother of vision."*
JAMES KOUZES AND BARRY POSNER

SO MANY OF US DOUBT OUR PRECOGNITIVE ABILITIES. I cannot estimate the number of times I have left the house and felt I had forgotten something only to discern thirty minutes later that I had. I've finally learned to trust my extrasensory memory. Now when I sense something is amiss, I stop, think, and look. One's extrasensory abilities are continually sending mental signals concerning decision making, safety, and recall. We literally have to train ourselves to trust these sensings. Many times it comes in the form of a hunch, something we are not trained to appreciate. Entrepreneurs are best at pursuing their hunches, although the successful ones probably do not refer to them as hunches. Professional

129

judgment, intuition, gut feeling, instinct, and inner voice are applicable descriptors. Whatever they are called, I suspect they use them as take off points for cost-benefit analysis and subsequent decisions to move forward.

Many never learn to trust their intuitive right brain. They are reluctant to place their success or failure at the foot of a hunch. Likewise, they do not want to be viewed as a "loose cannon." If they should fail, they want plenty of evidence that they thoroughly researched the issue before they ventured a decision. Unfortunately, many have become C.Y.A. managers and leaders.

Gerald Jackson in his *Executive ESP*, wrote of our failure to trust our intuitive abilities. "One such obstacle is over-reliance on the rational mind. Remember the Edsel? The Ford Motor Company has never lived down that design disaster back in the 50s. It remains the symbol of logical thinking unaided by inspiration. What research was done, what studies made! As a gesture toward the intuitive side of the brain, the company actually hired a poet, Marianne Moore, to come up with a name for the car. But in the end, the company ignored her suggestions...."

Ralph Larsen, chair and CEO of Johnson & Johnson, claims that failure to listen to his instincts has caused some bad decisions. He explains that 11 years at Johnson & Johnson taught him the importance of trusting his intuition. According to Larsen, senior management deals with issues too complex and ambiguous for quantitative decision-making. That is when the intuitive senior leader with the knowledge and intuitive skills earns his big salary.

Winners trust their instincts. Hayaski, writing for the *Harvard Business* Review, tells us that, "They hear the quiet alarms sounded by their intuitive brain. They investigate and act on the possibilities presented by these instincts. They are alert for signals of opportunities waiting to be seized." In spite of intuition and a bias for truth, we have become subservient to the political correctness model. Many are petrified by confrontation. Force of personality and a strongly voiced conviction or passion for a particular position may be frowned upon in group settings. I find this particularly true in educational settings. In a previous assignment in higher education, I could hardly hide my contempt for the unwillingness of administrators to disagree with some of the ludicrous positions taken by faculty relative to governance and student learning issues.

Real leaders trust their instincts and speak of them with passion and conviction. They will confront and disagree with diplomacy but nonetheless, they will always confront and disagree using judgment and forethought. They know that others will forgive errors in judgment but not ill motive.

SECTION 44

⎯⎯⎯⎯⎯

THOUGHTS ON EFFICIENCY

*"I've learned that you shouldn't have a $1,000 meeting
to solve a $100 problem."*
H. J. BROWN

*"A person who has not done one-half his day's work by ten o'clock,
runs a chance of leaving the other half undone."*
EMILY BRONTË

THE ACADEMICS WILL HARANGUE ME UNMERCIFULLY FOR ADDRESSING A SUBJECT SO BROAD IN SUCH A SHORT SECTION. And, of course, efficiency and effectiveness are too broad to adequately cover without significant research, but I am going to touch on a few areas that have caused me heartburn in my years.

Recently, in a prospering fitness center I saw a poster that said, "Happy Hour Starts at 5:00 AM!" This particular center opened its doors at 5:00 AM and the owner understood the importance of not only getting an early start himself but of catering to his customers who shared his "get things done mentality." Often, when others ask my opinion of the previous night's late show, I wonder how they think they can be sharp and on the mark the following day without the rest their bodies and minds require.

132

The fact is most aren't ready to face the next day. They sleep a little later, go to the office and immediately must field the telephone calls and electronic mail without any time to organize their day. Hence, they are continually in the catch-up mode, stressed out to the maximum, and finally go home distressed and remark how much they dislike their job. There is no substitute for a 5:00 AM happy hour filled with devotions, exercise, solitude, morning coffee, and a day organized before the first call is ever taken.

So much has been written about the conduct and organization of meetings. I don't even like to talk about meetings except to say that too many are inconsistent with efficient operations. A requirement for meetings clearly exists but in many contemporary organizations, the business day revolves around one meeting after another. When this is the case, efficiency takes a dive. Meetings invariably take too long particularly when chaired by the boss who is an extrovert at heart and loves to hear himself pontificate. Some of my most frustrating moments have been spent at the behest of colonels replete with "war stories" and egos that Idi Amin would be hard pressed to match. And worse, many of the meetings were designated "staff coordination." Generally, a requirement for staff coordination meetings does exist so that the right knows what the left is up to. But this can usually be accomplished weekly in a short update, which is chaired and clocked by one sympathetic to the time constraints of the staff.

Many bosses use meetings to pass out verbal taskers to the staff and quite frankly this works well for some. However, I am a firm believer in written taskers that provide some background, the task at hand, and the due date. This method is definitely impersonal; but it gives the action officer a record of exactly what is required and when. It is time sensitive because it can be delivered without waiting for the next meeting. With the advent of electronic mail, many are using written taskers but others still insist on the spoken word. The spoken word is exemplary of inefficiency in itself. It is subject to misinterpretation, poor hearing, and it cannot be reread for clarity.

I am not totally down on meetings in general. As stated above, a weekly staff meeting is beneficial. Additionally, a short meeting to "jump start" an action or project is useful particularly if the staff needs a warning order to prepare for a more formal tasker or to lay out the division of labor necessary to complete a forthcoming project.

The real morale busters are the 4:00 PM meetings, especially if they are on Fridays! Hubbard's Law, according to a collection of aphorisms by Jerry Gaither, says "The world gets a little better each morning, then worse again in the evening. Hold planning committee meetings in the morning."

Don't deal in multiple meetings. They all too frequently lead to personal interaction vice action. If executives in an organization spend more than a fairly small part of their time in meetings, it is a sure sign or malorganization.

More and more, I am realizing the value of time as a resource. Time is discussed to some degree in the section on procrastination; but I believe a comment on time as a resource are in order. Ben Franklin has told us, "If time be of all things the most precious, wasting time must be the greatest prodigality."

SECTION 45

HIRING WINNERS

*"Winners are quick to recognize faint praise
in prospective employee references."*
JIM BENSON

WHEN SEARCHING FOR CAPABLE PEOPLE WHO HAVE STAR QUALITY, WINNERS PAY LITTLE ATTENTION TO RÉSUMÉS. Since the candidate probably wrote or at least provided the information for the résumé, it has little value except to examine the quality and attention to detail in the résumé itself. Although the résumé may reflect experience, it may not define the quality of the experience. That is why winners move quickly to the references.

Winners recognize faint praise in a reference. References that attest to a candidate's punctuality and low absenteeism and even worse, state that the candidate is a good worker, will cause that application to end up in the dead file. Winners are searching for statements that describe star quality such as outstanding, remarkable, incredible, one of a kind, and committed. Once the winner finds a candidate whose references reflect that kind of star quality, he starts looking for a job fit. Does this person have other credentials that make him a fit for this position or another within the organization? According to Harvey Mackay, once you find a man of star quality, you hire him even if you don't have a place for him.

SECTION 46

PUBLIC SPEAKING

"Extemporaneous speaking should be practiced and cultivated."
ABRAHAM LINCOLN

"Speakers are only as good
as the material they prepare and deliver."
JIM BENSON

SPEAKERS ARE ONLY AS GOOD AS THE MATERIAL THEY PREPARE AND
DELIVER. The winner never ceases to collect material.
Generally, the best speakers are well read individuals—oth-
erwise, where would they collect their material?

Experienced speakers save anecdotes, stories, quotes,
facts, openers, and closers in subject files. They highlight
personal books making notes in the margins facilitating future reference. Additionally, they keep a notebook in their
car to jot down thoughts and ideas of value while traveling to and from work. Over the years their collections are
replete with information on topics of choice enabling them
to quickly prepare a speech. Their best material is used
over and over with different audiences.

Rarely do experienced speakers give extemporaneous presentations, because they anticipate and are virtually always prepared. Sometimes preparation is only in the mind when very short notice speaking requirements arise. Usually, the tried and true openers and closers are readily available.

Good speakers rehearse their presentations to define their pauses and inflection. It is alright to refer to notes but unacceptable to read a speech. The amount of study and rehearsal will dictate how much the speaker refers to his notes. The less—the better.

SECTION 47

CLOSURE

"You can, you will, you must succeed."
RAYMOND A. BUSSARD

AS YOUNG LEADERS, "YOU CAN, YOU WILL, YOU MUST" BE READY TO TAKE OVER AS THE NEXT LEADERS OF OUR COUNTRY. "You can, you will, you must" be ethical and well prepared decision-makers—leaders who are grounded in values that cause you to choose the harder right over the easier wrong—every time. "You can, you will, you must succeed," because our country is depending on you.

On February 11, 1861, Abraham Lincoln spoke to the people of Springfield, Illinois who had gathered at the railroad station to see him off to Washington, D.C.:

"...without the assistance of that Divine Being, who ever attended him, I cannot succeed. With that assistance I cannot fail. Trusting in him, who can go with me, and remain with you and be everywhere for good, let us confidently hope that all will yet be well. To his care commending you, as I hope in your prayers you will commend me, I bid you an affectionate farewell."

BIBLIOGRAPHY

Bennis, Warren and Nanus, Burt. *Leaders: The Strategies for Taking Charge*

Brown, Steven. *13 Fatal Errors Managers Make and How You Can Avoid Them*

Carnegie, Dale. *How to Develop Confidence and Influence People by Public Speaking*

Carnegie, Dale. *How to Win Friends and Influence People*

Carter, Steven. *Integrity*

Cockell, Lee. *"Creating Magic"*

Daniel, T. L. "Managerial Behavior: Their Relationship to Perceived Organizational Climate in a High-Technology Company." *Group and Organizational Studies*

Drucker, Peter. *The Effective Executive*

Dunnan, Maxie. "Christians Under Construction and in Recovery." *Upper Room Books*

Franklin, Benjamin. *Benjamin Franklin, the Autobiography and Other Writings*

Garder, John. *On Leadership*

Gineen, Harold. *Managing*

Hayaski, A. M. *When to Trust Your Gut*

Henil, R. D., Jr. *Dictionary of Military and Naval Quotations*

Hilton, Conrad. *Be My Guest*

Jackson, Gerald. *Executive ESP*

Knight, Bobby. *His Own Man*

Kriegel, Robert J. and Patler, Louis. *If it Ain't Broke...Break it*

Mackay, Harvey. *Beware the Naked Man Who Offers You His Shirt*

Mackay, Harvey. *Swim With the Sharks*

McCormick, Mark. *What They Don't Teach You at the Harvard Business School*

Mintzberg, Henry and Quinn, James. *The Strategy Process*

O'Brien, Michael. *Vince*

Paterno, Joe. *Paterno: By the Book*

Peters, Tom and Austin, Nancy. *A Passion for Excellence*

Phillips, Donald T. *Lincoln on Leadership*

Pierce, Richard. *Leadership Perspective, and Restructuring for Total Quality*

Pollard, C. William. *The Soul of the Firm*

Riley, Pat. *The Winner Within*

Ringer, Robert. *Million Dollar Habits*

Roberts, Wess. *Leadership Secrets of Attila the Hun*

Staples, Walter D. *Think Like a Winner*

Stieglitz, H. "Chief Executives View Their Jobs: Today and Tomorrow." *Conference Board Report*

Stockdale, James. "Educating Leaders." *The Washington Quarterly*

Thomas, Dave. *Well Done*

Townsend, Robert. *Up the Organization*

Trulock, Alice R. *In the Hands of Providence*

Waitley, Denis. *Empires of the Mind*

Walsh, Bill. *Building a Champion*

Walton, Mary. *The Deming Management Method*

Ziglar, Zig. *Over the Top*

ABOUT THE AUTHOR

DR. JAMES H. BENSON, SR., COLONEL, UNITED STATES MARINE CORPS (RETIRED), IS THE 8TH PRESIDENT OF RIVERSIDE MILITARY ACADEMY. He became the 15th president of Marion Military Institute, Marion, Alabama on July 15, 2004. Colonel Benson retired from the Marine Corps in 1995 and subsequently served as

Executive Assistant to the President and Director of Planning and as Vice President for Administration at Bridgewater College, Virginia from March, 1995 until July, 2004.

Colonel Benson received a Bachelor of Arts degree from Bridgewater College and holds a Master of Science Degree from the University of Tennessee, a Master of Public Administration Degree from Penn State University, and completed his doctorate in Higher Education Administration at The George Washington University. Colonel Benson is also a graduate of the Armed Forces Staff College and the Army War College.

Colonel Benson's military career included assignments as Commanding Officer, JTF-129, Special Operations Counter-terrorism Joint Task Force; Commanding Officer, Sixth Marine Regiment; and Chief of Staff/Assistant Division Commander of the Second Marine Division. He is a decorated combat veteran of the Vietnam War. Colonel Benson was awarded the Defense Superior Service Medal, three Legion of Merit Awards, two Bronze Stars with "V" for Valor, the Meritorious Service Medal, the Joint Service Commendation Medal, the Vietnamese Cross of Gallantry with Palm, three Navy Commendation Medals, one with "V" for Valor, and the Navy Achievement Medal.

Colonel Benson and his wife Mary have a daughter, Catherine R. Benson, graduate of George Mason University, and a son, James H. Benson II, graduate of Eastern Mennonite University.

"An outstanding practical guide
based on the author's long experience.
It will assist aspiring young men and women to understand
the art and science of influence
and to develop their personal leadership.
America and the free world crave positive leadership.
Here is a superb primer."

"...I can certainly see where this (book)
will be beneficial to future military leaders,
business owners, athletes, academic faculty and staff.
It is very well done."